Living Victoriously with Anxiety and Depression

Loice Robi Byler
with Esther Good

FreedomInHimMinistries

Published by Freedom in Him Ministries
www.FreedomInHimMinistries.com

Copyright 2013 © by Loice Robi Byler
All rights reserved. No part of this book may be reproduced or transmitted in any form or by any means, electronic or mechanical, including photocopying and recording, or by any information storage and retrieval system, without permission in writing from the publisher.

Scripture taken from the HOLY BIBLE, NEW INTERNATIONAL VERSION®. Copyright © 1973, 1978, 1984 Biblica. Used by permission of Zondervan. All rights reserved.

The "NIV" and "New International Version" trademarks are registered in the United States Patent and Trademark Office by Biblica. Use of either trademark requires the permission of Biblica.

ISBN-13: 978-0-9890043-0-5
ISBN-10: 0989004309

For my loving husband Jon, who has stood by me, encouraged me, and walked this journey in the good times and in the bad times. Thank you for helping me come to a place of wholeness.

Contents

FOREWORD..7

INTRODUCTION..11

PART 1: MY STORY

    CHAPTER 1: THE EARLY YEARS 17

    CHAPTER 2: THE COLLEGE YEARS 25

    CHAPTER 3: AFTER COLLEGE..39

    CHAPTER 4: THE WEDDING...51

    CHAPTER 5: BECOMING PARENTS 57

    CHAPTER 6: BACK TO KENYA 63

    CHAPTER 7: BUILDING A HOUSE 73

    CHAPTER 8: VICTOR, NOT VICTIM................................77

PART 2: UNDERSTANDING ANXIETY AND DEPRESSION

    CHAPTER 9: ANXIETY 83

    CHAPTER 10: DEPRESSION 87

    CHAPTER 11: SEASONAL AFFECTIVE DISORDER 93

Chapter 12: Suicide 95
Chapter 13: Medication 99
Chapter 14: Triggers 103

PART 3: THE JOURNEY TO WHOLENESS

Chapter 15: The Power of God's Love 109
Chapter 16: The Power of Forgiveness...............119
Chapter 17: The Power of Praise 135
Chapter 18: The Power of the Word 141
Chapter 19: The Power of Words 157
Chapter 20: The Power of Prayer........................161
Chapter 21: Encouragers 169
Chapter 22: Weapons to Fight
    Anxiety and Depression................................173
Chapter 23: Living Victoriously 183

WORKS CITED 191

ACKNOWLEDGEMENTS 193

ABOUT THE AUTHOR 195

ABOUT FREEDOM IN HIM MINISTRIES 197

Foreword

Satan has long used the secrecy and shame surrounding anxiety and depression to keep God's beloved children sitting in darkness. Enough is enough!

For over 20 years I have watched, sometimes up close and sometimes from a distance, as my Aunt Loice Robi Byler has lived the journey she has written about in these pages. She is authentic. And I can testify that she is whole. While she at times desperately cries out to others for prayer, she just as often moves toward others to pray for them. She visits the sick, bakes birthday cakes for those who wouldn't have any, creates "church" weekly in a neglected apartment building, and preaches God's word from the pulpit, over the phone and to her own heart! She has told me what I needed to hear many times, whether I wanted to or not!

This woman lives life on God's mission. Yet she does it *with* anxiety and depression.

This book is not a quick-fix for those struggling with anxiety and depression because there is no quick fix. It is the story of a godly woman struggling hard, falling, and getting back up in the strength that Jesus and His community of support around her provide. It is a courageous invitation into an imperfect woman's world. It is a testimony of Jesus' daily victory and strength in the lifelong fight for full freedom.

Can Jesus completely remove anxiety and depression? Definitely. Does he sometimes wait until heaven? Definitely. And we don't know why.

Aunt Loice holds the tension of waiting for complete healing from a hated disease and yet living victoriously today better than anyone I know.

As I live life as an encourager, friend, and pastor to women, I'm excited to get my hands on this printed book, both to better understand how to encourage those dealing with anxiety and depression and to place it in the hands of those currently in the midst of the struggle.

May Jesus use this powerful declaration to release those currently sitting in darkness out into the full sunlight of greater Freedom in Him!

-Melanie (Byler) Nofziger, wife, mother, friend and pastor…also on the journey to full freedom in Him.

Melanie (Byler) Nofziger is an associate pastor at North Clinton Mennonite Church in Wauseon, Ohio.

Introduction

After I had been diagnosed with anxiety and depression, I read book after book on the subject. Each time, I would think I had found the key to overcoming anxiety and depression. Although it may work that way for some people, for me it continued to be a struggle. This was a very frustrating process because I would have such high hopes, thinking I had found the answer, only to come back down again, hurting from anxiety and depression. I started feeling like the Apostle Paul in 2 Corinthians 12:7, who, though he begged God and prayed, the thorn in his flesh was not removed. I realized that my journey was not to overcome anxiety and depression, but to live victoriously in spite of it. 2 Corinthians 2:14 reads, "But thanks be to God, who always leads us in triumphal procession in Christ and through us spreads everywhere the fragrance of the knowledge of him." God always leads us in triumphal procession, even if we continue to struggle.

I want to share my story with you because I believe that God does not waste pain. He is a Redeemer and He redeems even those things we would rather do without. Romans 8:28 says, "And we know that in all things God works for the good of those who love Him, who have been called according to his purpose." One of the ways that God has redeemed my pain is by allowing me to start Freedom In Him Ministries to reach out to others, especially those struggling with anxiety and depression. The purpose of my ministry is to touch the lives of women who share these struggles and open doors for those who are fighting the battle quietly to have a place to share.

A lot of women who are hurting feel alone and it is such a blessing for us to be able to sit and share our struggles, knowing that the other person understands. Sharing with someone who understands anxiety and depression from his or her own experience, rather than from studying a textbook, can be both therapeutic and liberating. I invite you to enter my journey and know that you are not alone in your struggles. I hope and pray that it will be a safe place for you.

Part 1

My Story

Chapter 1

The Early Years

I grew up in Nakuru, Kenya as the eldest of eight children. My Dad had a good job as a store manager in a car dealership and my mom was always running some small business, from selling used clothes or buying and reselling cooking fat, to selling greens from her garden. Our needs were provided for and I had a happy childhood.

I did not have problems with anxiety and depression as a child, but looking back, I recognize things in my life that foreshadowed the struggle ahead. I was always much smaller than the other kids. The bigger girls mothered me and when we would play house, I was always the child or baby. At home, I struggled with the fear of not being good enough and felt anxious when my dad would leave for work. My mother never disciplined us until he was gone, so in my mind I associated his leaving with being disciplined. I also remember being frightened of my grandmother. She had the reputation of being strangely fickle. One minute she was sweet and delightful, and the next she was in your face, angrily shaking her finger at you. Now, after my continuing struggle, I recognize the symptoms of a mental health disorder. I wish we had known more about these issues then, so she could have had help and support.

We always attended church and Sunday school. I had a Sunday school teacher whom I adored. I thought she was beautiful and sweet, and hoped I would be just like her when I grew up. At the age of ten, most kids would stand up in church and commit their lives to Jesus. They would then attend Catechism class, get baptized, receive a new name. I followed the same pattern, and when I was baptized, I chose the name Rose. My dad didn't like the name, so he changed my name to Loice, which I still use today.

I enjoyed school and walked to the school in the neighborhood wearing the same red and white uniform as the other girls. I always wanted to be a teacher, and in the evenings, after we had all done our homework, the kids in our row of houses would gather around a street lamp to play school. In the fading light, they would all sit on the ground in rows in front of me, and I would pretend to teach them, reviewing math problems or English words that I had learned earlier that day. We stayed there playing long after the sun set, until our parents finally called us in for supper.

I never lost my desire to teach, so when I graduated from high school, I went to teacher's college. After college, I received a certificate for teaching elementary school and began working. Fresh out of teacher's college, I was much more motivated than many of the teachers at my school who had been working for years. I wrote detailed lesson plans for each day and strictly followed the curriculum. As part of the required curriculum, I had my class build a small town out of boxes with a small garden in the middle of it. My class was the only one in the whole school to finish the project and I was so proud of it. The children would pretend to farm in the miniature town, and discuss what crops they were growing.

Since my family's home was so far from the school, I lived on the school compound in a small, one room cement hut with a tin roof. I went home to visit as often as I could, but on weekends when I couldn't make the trip, one of my brothers or sisters would come to visit me and bring my mail and a sack of produce from my mom's vegetable garden. They enjoyed taking the public transportation, or *matatu,* out to my school, and saw the visit to their older sister as a treat.

I enjoyed my work, but wanted to get further training in Christian Ministry. At that time, my father was involved in a group that supported and educated farmers about growing their gardens, or *shambas*. The group received support from someone in the U.S. who was from the same denomination. Through this individual, the opportunity opened up for four people from our community to attend Belhaven College, in Jackson Mississippi, and I was one of the four chosen to go.

I was excited to be chosen, and knew this was my opportunity to receive further training in Christian Ministry. However, the idea seemed distant and almost unattainable, so I continued my life as usual. On one of the weekends when I hadn't planned to go home, my brother was sent to visit me. I wrapped up my lesson plans and notes on Saturday morning just before he arrived. When he got there, we went to my hut and I sat on my bed and started to sift through the mail that had piled up for me while I was away. My heart started pounding when I noticed a crisp white envelope with American stamps. I quickly slit open the flap and pulled out the contents. It was my I-20 immigration form to study at Belhaven College. It took a moment for the reality to sink in. Just minutes earlier, traveling to the U.S. for school had seemed like a fragile dream, and suddenly it was a reality.

I squealed with joy and shook the letter in my brother's face. It took him a minute to decipher what I was so excited about, but he laughed and listened as I excitedly started to plan. I couldn't keep the news to myself, so I made a quick lunch, and then we both headed home on the next *matatu*. My family was surprised to see us when we walked up to the house later that day.

"I thought you weren't coming home this weekend," my mother said.

I just grinned and held out my letter to her. "It's my I-20!" I said. "This means I'm really going to America to study!"

A few weeks later, my dad took me to Nairobi to get my passport. Once we had it, we headed over to the U.S. Embassy to get my visa. When we walked up to the embassy, the guard told us that it was closed for an American holiday. Instead of taking the long trip home, we spent the night with my uncle who lived in Nairobi, and the next morning, bright and early, we headed to the embassy again. This time, a line had already formed when we got there, full of people hopeful to walk away with a visa. Once we were inside, waiting to be called, I couldn't help but overhear frustrated conversations as person after person was denied a visa. Occasionally, someone's appointment went without incident, but time after time, I saw people leaving frustrated or dejected. A sinking feeling grew in my stomach as I anxiously waited for my name to be called.

When it was finally my turn, I walked hesitantly up to the window. I passed my passport, I-20, and all my other documents through the slot to the person on the other side, and explained my situation. I held my breath as the immigration officer reviewed my paperwork, afraid that something might go wrong. She simply asked me to pay for the visa and told me to pick up my passport that afternoon. I could hardly believe it later that day when my passport was handed back to me, now including a student visa for America. It was done. I was approved. I was really going!

Our spirits were high as we left the embassy and headed to the *matatu* stop. My father spontaneously stopped at a small kiosk along the way and purchased a big khaki green suitcase for me. I was honored at his thoughtful gift. Not only was it the most expensive gift I had ever been given, it also made my approaching trip seem all the more real.

The next few months passed by in a flurry of excitement as we made plans and preparations. I received constant congratulations and well wishes from family and friends at church. To raise money for my plane ticket, the women of the community cooked a meal. We invited family and friends and everyone in the community. The money from the meal put a big dent into the formidable amount we needed to come up with, and slowly but surely, everything fell into place.

I went shopping for new clothes. Since I was going to the U.S., my dad relaxed his rule about wearing only skirts and dresses, so I bought a few pairs of slacks as well. On the day I left, I wore one of my new outfits, a green shirt with a velvet skirt and matching vest. I had my hair done and I felt ready to face the world.

Friends and family all came along with us to drop me off at the airport. I was both nervous and elated at the exciting new opportunity before me, and my heightened emotions made the many goodbyes all the more difficult. I could hardly bear to leave them, but the knowledge that we would see each other again carried us through. When I had said all of my goodbyes, I turned and walked towards my gate, little knowing the challenges that lay ahead.

Chapter 2

The College Years

I encountered my first obstacle before I had even boarded the plane – an escalator. I had never seen one before, and expected it to stop moving so that I could step on, but it kept right on going. I stood there watching it for what seemed like hours, when suddenly a stranger grabbed my bag and took my hand and helped me on. When we reached the top, he helped me off, gave me my bag, and walked in the other direction. I was a little flustered, but thankful to that Good Samaritan for helping me in my time of need.

By the time I finally reached the gate, they had already announced the final boarding call and were looking for me because I was the last one to board. Relieved, I made my way to my seat for my first plane ride; adrenaline was still coursing through me from being late. I tried to strike up a conversation with the girl next to me, but she wasn't interested in talking, so I settled in for the ride.

We landed in West Africa, where I boarded my flight to New York. When I arrived in New York, I was overwhelmed. The airport was huge and there were signs pointing in every direction. I saw a man in a uniform, and asked him for help finding my gate. I showed him the information on my ticket, and he proceeded into what I assumed to be a series of directions for how to get where I was going. The only problem was that I couldn't understand a word he was saying. I was pretty sure it was English, because he had no trouble understanding me, but I was used to an academic, British English, and wasn't prepared for the thick accent of a native New Yorker. I smiled, thanked him for his help, and walked confidently in the direction he had pointed, hoping that whatever directions he had given me weren't too complicated.

I finally found the flight headed for Mississippi—the final leg of my journey. When I got off the plane, clothing crumpled and eyes scratchy from lack of sleep, I was relieved to see two of the other Kenyan students who had come before me waiting to pick me up. Two Americans were with them, and everyone gave me a hug, including the guys. That was a shock because in Kenya men and women don't traditionally hug each other.

On our way to the school, we stopped to get fast food. We went in, and the others ordered for me, since I didn't know what most of the food was. I recognized the French fries, though we called them *chips* in Kenya. The burger, on the other hand, looked suspicious. I lifted the bun and found a yellow square of gooey mess melted over the meat. *I'll never eat that*, I thought to myself. I had never seen cheese like that before.

When I first arrived at the college, I was struck by the deep green of the manicured lawns that carpeted the entire campus. Even the trees and shrubs were uncommonly plump and round and bursting with life. It was so different from home, where the various shades of greens and tawny browns ebbed and flowed with the rainy and dry seasons, and gangly trees randomly dotted the landscape.

As I began school and my life in the U.S. simultaneously, I had a lot of adjusting to do. I fell asleep during class due to jetlag, and watched in awe as the grocery store doors opened automatically. It took me a long time to get used to the public displays of affection that were so taboo in Kenya, where displays of affection were always a very private thing. Even the social customs were different. One time I was approaching a classroom door when the teacher, laden with books, got there at the same time. In my culture, the teacher should have entered first because he was an elder and because he was carrying books, but he stopped at the doorway, and said, "After you." I tried to argue for him to go first, but he insisted, saying, "Ladies first." It was a funny incident with each of us trying to get the other to go first out of our cultural norms.

I had an especially hard time getting used to the cafeteria. I was surprised not only by the amount and variety of food, but also by the way it was laid out for us to pick and choose what we wanted. I paid special attention to the foods that my Kenyan friends took, and followed behind them, taking the same things, and hoping

I would like them. On shrimp night, I noticed that none of my friends would take any shrimp. I took one look at them and decided I wouldn't risk it either. Later on when I finally tried it, I found that I actually love shrimp!

Our dorm mother had an arrangement with some people in the community who would call her if they needed a babysitter and she would find someone to babysit for them. If any of the girls in the dorm wanted babysitting jobs, they signed up with her. This was a very good system because it gave the girls a way to make a little money. I had many cultural "bloopers" every time I tried something new, and babysitting was no exception.

One time, when I babysat for a local family, the mother asked me to make a peanut butter sandwich for her daughter. I pictured the sandwiches I had seen, stacked high with meat, lettuce and tomatoes. I assumed that proportion of bread to "stuffing" was standard, so I proceeded to pile an inch of peanut butter onto the bread. The girl's father was watching and his eyes kept getting bigger and bigger as I added on the layers of peanut butter, but he never said anything. Now looking back, I feel bad for the poor girl who had to eat that sandwich. She could have choked!

Not only did I have a hard time adjusting to all the new things I encountered, but others also reacted to me. When I came from Kenya, I had my hair done in an elaborate weave that was common at the time. When I came to the U.S., it was seen as an anomaly. Most people didn't understand what a weave was, and assumed that each day I braided my hair into the elaborate arrangement they saw on my head. Others asked if I took it off every night. I laughed at this, thinking of the hours it had taken to put in. If I did that every day, I would have no time for classes! In the grocery store, strangers would come up to me and ask if they could touch my hair. I wasn't used to being the center of so much attention.

Eventually, I became more comfortable in my surroundings and began to make friends. My roommate was a beautiful Ethiopian girl who loved to laugh, so we connected right away because we were both experiencing similar adjustments. We loved to sit outside the dorm and enjoy the fresh air and talk.

It was while I was at college that I learned to truly own my faith. I have always been grateful for my Christian upbringing, which laid a solid foundation for my faith. But at home, I had always had the support of friends and family who encouraged me in my faith. I went to church because it was the natural thing to do. I had always gone to church with my family

Even in areas of faith I struggled with culture shock,. One day, after I had attended a church service, I walked outside to find some elders of the church gathered around smoking. Elders in Kenya would never have done that as it was strictly considered to be a sin. I went back to the dorm and told my friend, "I am never going to church in America again!" She tried to talk to me about it, but nothing she said made me feel any better.

Finally I found a professor to talk to. I explained the situation to him, and he was very understanding of the dilemma I was facing. He convinced me that not all of the elders smoked. When I accepted this fact, I realized that I would have to go back to church. After all, I was going to be here for several years and I couldn't just worship alone for that whole time.

Even though I was attending a Christian college, I was soon being pulled in two directions. One group of people was inviting me to join them as they went to the disco to party, while the other group spent their free time in extracurricular activities like the Missions Fellowship. One night, when I was torn between joining a party with my friends or staying in the dorm, I heard God say, "Loice, your mom and dad aren't here now. You need to decide for yourself. Will you choose the disco, or the church?" Although I had become a Christian years before, that was a defining moment for me. I knelt beside my bed and made the commitment to follow Jesus. I have never looked back.

Eventually, I began to make friends who were committed to their faith and encouraged me in mine. One such friend was the most beautiful, soft spoken woman I had ever met. We immediately hit it off, and quickly became good friends. She was going through a lot in her family at the time, and we frequently met and prayed together. One day in my dorm room after we had prayed, we were chatting about our classes and friends.

"Oh, I met this really nice girl the other day. She also has a really cute brother," she said with a cheeky grin and a wink. "I think they're Mennonite."

I didn't know who Mennonites were, but I knew who Mormons were and quickly associated the two in my mind. I thought to myself, *That's wonderful that these Mormons came here to a Christian school. What a great opportunity to reach them.* So I began to fervently pray for this brother and sister to get saved. Little did I know that they were already saved, and that I was praying for the man who would later become my husband! Later, I would tease him, saying that I prayed for his salvation.

I eventually met Jon, since we were both Christian Ministries majors. He was very reserved and quiet. We had many classes together, and he would always arrive first and sit alone. I often came in with a cluster of girls, always talking and giggling. We would all say, "Hi Jon!" and he would blush and quietly greet us. I began to see him in more of my classes. One time during a class, the teacher asked us to turn to the person sitting beside us and tell them what we would be doing ten years from that day. Jon happened to be sitting beside me, and I told him that I would be raising my ten children. Apparently it didn't scare him off!

Jon and I got to know each other better through a mutual friend who was a quadriplegic. I often ate lunch with him, and since he wasn't able to carry his own tray, I would fill and carry an extra tray for him and spoon feed him. Jon often picked up the same friend and drove him to school, so he began to sit with us at lunch as well.

Our friend was a jokester and I was easily embarrassed by his teasing. One time when he pointed out a run in my panty hose, I was so embarrassed I wanted to sink through the floor. Even though I was always embarrassed by his teasing, he always knew how to make us smile.

Soon I began going with Jon when he drove to pick up and drop off our friend each day. On the way back, we would have time to talk, and through all our time together, we began to develop an interest in each other. The change came gradually, but I found myself anticipating the next time I would see him and thinking about him when he wasn't around.

I was elated when Jon finally approached me to talk about the possibility of a relationship because it confirmed that he was feeling the same things I was feeling. We decided to take a weekend apart from each other to pray and reflect, and then meet afterwards to decide if we should date. After the weekend apart, we agreed we felt God's blessing to move forward in our relationship.

Jon and I attended the Student Mission Fellowship that was held at the home of a teacher and his wife. Their home was always open to students and I even stayed with them during school breaks and summers when the dorms were closed. From 7:00 p.m. to 9:00 p.m. every Thursday evening during the school year, we came together for singing, prayer, and teaching or discussion. Ten or fifteen of us would pack into the room, filling the chairs and the floor. After Jon and I started dating, he would walk me back to the dorm when the Student Mission Fellowship was over.

As our relationship began to get more serious, Jon invited me to go with him to the church that he and his sisters attended. Teasing, I replied, "I need a written invitation." To my surprise, the next day, I received the following note in the campus mail.

The bearer of this certificate is hereby cordially invited to worship with the believers at Open Door Mennonite Church, 2023 W. Capitol St. This offer is valid for any of the regular gatherings of the above mentioned group, including the 10:00am service on Sunday and the Small Group Fellowship on Wednesday evening. Transportation will be provided upon request. RSVP

I happily accepted, and as I attended Jon's church, I got to know his sisters. They were very warm and inviting and made me feel comfortable and welcome. Jon lived with his younger sister Jody, so I visited their house frequently. One time when Jon and Jody both had to be away, they asked me to watch the house for them.

I asked Jody, "Is there anything I can do for you while you're away?" She thought for a moment and said, "Well, you could make some cookies if you want."

I agreed to make cookies for her, and the moment they were gone I set out to start. I didn't grow up baking cookies, but I had made them before while babysitting for another family, and I knew it was quite simple. All I had to do was find the tube of cookie dough, and follow the instructions. I searched through the entire refrigerator and freezer, but couldn't find the dough anywhere. When Jon and Jody got home, I said, "I'm sorry. I couldn't make cookies because I couldn't find the cookie dough." When they realized that I had been looking for ready-made dough, they both had a good laugh. For them, baking cookies from scratch had been a regular part of growing up. It never occurred to them that I wouldn't have had the same experience.

The first time Jon's parents came to visit after we had started dating, Jon brought me over to the house to meet them. I was so nervous, but the moment I walked through the door, everyone said, "Hi, Loice!" Jon's mother walked over to me and wrapped her arms around me, and gave me a big squeeze. She made me feel so welcome and accepted and my anxiety melted away.

Chapter 3

After College

When we graduated from college, Jon joined a missions group in Oregon. After serving in Oregon for several months, the group traveled across the country, making stops along the way. Before he left Oregon, he gave me the addresses of every stop he would make along the way so that I could write to him and he would have letters waiting all the way from Oregon to New York where their team would eventually settle.

While Jon moved to Oregon, I stayed in Jackson, moved in with his sister and began working for a program for ex-offenders and young African American boys. The program I worked with helped the ex-offenders to find homes and jobs and at the same time, mentored the younger boys by showing them the hard road ahead for those who end up entangled in the legal system. We also spent time in juvenile detention centers visiting the young men. We mostly sat and listened, but we always offered to pray with them and tried to offer encouragement for them to turn their lives around. I enjoyed my time in the program and learned a lot, but couldn't help being frustrated by feeling that we could be doing more with the resources we had to work with.

Jon and I called each other every week and wrote letters back and forth frequently. When the year was finally over, Jon came back for a short visit, and then moved to New York. One day, while we were on the phone, he surprised me by asking me to marry him. I was so shocked, I couldn't say anything. I sat in silence on the phone for several moments. I'm sure he wondered what I was thinking. After I had time to digest what he had asked me, I knew what my answer would be and I joyfully accepted.

I wrote a letter to my dad, telling him about Jon and that we were interested in getting married. My dad wrote back saying, "In our culture, these are things you discuss with your mother, not your father. But, if this is what God wants, I'm sure it will work out." I took that as affirmation, and Jon and I went ahead with our engagement. My dad also said it was time for me to come home and I agreed. Jon continued to live in New York, as I finished up the year and went home to my family.

I was so happy to be back in Kenya, surrounded by friends and family. It took weeks just to visit everyone I needed to see since coming back. I felt surrounded by people who loved me. But when I brought up my engagement with my dad, his reaction was not at all what I had expected. Instead of being supportive and happy, he refused to give his consent.

In the mornings, I would get up and cook him his breakfast. He would seem congenial, and I thought he might be softening to the idea of Jon and I getting married. But by evening, when he came home, he was often in a sour mood again. I later learned that during the day when he met with his friends, some of them would taunt him, saying, "Are you really going to let your daughter marry a man you've never met?" Now that I am a parent, I understand all of the fears that must have been running through his head. He had no way of knowing what kind of man Jon was. But at the time, it made no sense to me.

The situation didn't get any better. My father was hoping that I would forget about marrying this stranger and settle down and get a job. I tried to look for work, but I didn't feel I could make a commitment since I didn't know how long it would be until I got married, or where Jon and I would live after that. Even though I made an effort, my heart wasn't in it because I was consumed with worry about my future with Jon.

My parents were building a house at the time on the side of a hill. The area was still being cleared and the construction had just begun. One day we were at the site of the new house, looking down over the valley below. The ground was covered in rocks and boulders, and some of the larger ones were being used to build the kitchen.

I decided to bring up the subject once again. I said, "What are you thinking about this marriage? Do you understand what I've been telling you? We are sure we want to get married. I've prayed about it like you asked me to, and I haven't changed my mind."

He got so angry that he kicked one of the large rocks so hard it dislodged from its place in the ground and rolled the whole way down the hill. I was completely downtrodden, and started to feel unwell. Sometimes panic would rise up in my chest and I would feel my heart begin to race. I went to visit Alice, one of my best friends who was going to be my maid of honor. When I got to the office where she worked, I collapsed into a chair.

"What's wrong?" she asked.

"I've been feeling so sick lately," I replied. "I'm tired all the time, and I can't sleep. I'm even starting to feel dizzy. Will you walk me to the doctor?"

She took a long look at me, and said, "Why don't we just sit here and talk for a minute."

Before I knew it, I was pouring my heart out to her. I had been hearing bits and pieces of gossip about what people were saying behind my back. Some people believed that Jon and I had already gotten married without my parents' permission, and that I was lying to them by saying we hadn't gotten married yet. It seemed that no matter how hard we tried to do the right thing, people still thought the worst.

Alice looked me in the eye and said, "Loice, you don't have to listen to any of that. You know the truth, and you don't have to entertain their gossip."

I thought, *she's right. I don't need the added stress of worrying about what everyone thinks.* It was like a huge weight had been lifted from me. A few days later, a young man came up to me and said, "Loice, have you heard what people are saying about you?"

I just shook my head and said, "It doesn't matter. I don't want to hear it." And from that point on, I refused to listen to the rumors, or let them dictate how I felt.

That was a time of a lot of prayer for all of us. Jon and I continued to communicate, and I knew that he would wait as long as it took to get my father's approval. My mom's best friend, who was also my mentor, encouraged me to pray and I came to the decision that even if I had to wait for ten years, I would still wait for Jon. My parents prayed over and over again, and finally, one day, my father asked, "Does that man still want to come to Kenya?"

I looked at him startled as hope started to bubble up in my chest. "Yes."

He looked hard at me, and then smiled, and said, "Tell him to come."

We were so excited to finally be able to get married. Jon made plans to come early so that he could get to know my family and community before the wedding. He arrived mid-summer and my family immediately accepted him. Jon and I had hoped to get married in August, but when we discussed the date with my father, he said it was too soon, so we set the date for November instead.

Once the date was set, the wedding preparations began in earnest. I had bought my dress in the U.S. before coming home, so Jon brought it with him when he came. We began making trips back and forth to Nairobi on the *matatu* to get material for the bridesmaids' dresses and other wedding supplies. One of my mother's friends was a seamstress, so she took care of sewing the dresses for all of the bridesmaids and flower girls.

My parents were still building their house, so Jon pitched in, and was quickly welcomed by the family and neighbors alike. As they worked side by side, Jon and my brother became good friends, and I felt overjoyed that not only had my father given his approval, but that my family had accepted Jon and welcomed him with open arms.

As the time neared for the wedding, Jon's parents, sister, and niece flew to Kenya for the wedding. We greeted them at the airport, and the next day, left for a safari. As we bumped along the rough paths in the game reserve, I remember Jon's mother, Fannie, standing up through the opening in the roof to watch for animals. Dressed in a long dress and Mennonite covering, she smiled as the wind blew in her face, and said, "Mm. Fannie Byler in Africa."

We slept in tents, and the cook had a makeshift kitchen set up around an open fire, We were amazed by the tasty dishes he managed to pull together. The first night we couldn't get to sleep until almost 2:00 a.m. because a group of young Europeans had just arrived and were noisily partying. For breakfast, we had some of the most delicious eggs I had ever tasted. In the evenings, we would all sit around the fire and listen to Jon's dad tell stories. The entire trip was such a great experience full of precious memories for the entire family.

Back in Nakuru, Jon's family fit in right away. They easily got along with everyone they met and relished being in another culture. Each family made concessions to accommodate the other culture. In my family's culture the groom's family traditionally pays a dowry to the bride's family. In Jon's culture, there was no official dowry, but Jon's parent's graciously agreed to the custom. So Jon and I sat down with our parents and another couple and worked out the details of the dowry. Traditionally, the bride would not have been involved, but we decided that given the melding of two cultures, I would be included in the discussion. It felt very uncomfortable to sit through a discussion about my own dowry.

It was a blessing to have Jon's sister Jody there for the wedding. She jumped right into the wedding preparation, and took responsibility for decorating the cake we had made. She even brought her own icing and decorating equipment from home. The bridesmaids' dresses were a light peach color and I had hoped to have the cake match, but each time Jody tried to dye the icing, it came out orange or pink. I was starting to feel disappointed that it wasn't going to work out, when she said, "Let me just try one more thing." So she took a little carrot juice, and mixed it into the white icing, and it blended to become the lovely shade of peach we had been aiming for.

During the final week before the wedding, a friend lent us his car, as we ran errands, picking up the men's suits and my dress from the drycleaner. Everyone in the community pitched in. Some families in the community came together to plan the meal for the reception and they decided how much food was needed. If they decided that they needed fifty kilos of rice, each family would step up and say, "I can bring one kilo," or, "I can bring three kilos," until they had fifty kilos. They went through each item on the menu until all of the food was covered.

The night before the wedding, all the women gathered at our house to peel potatoes and prepare the food for the next day. It is a common custom for the women who contributed to the wedding to ask the groom's family for a gift in return and sometimes this can delay the wedding for hours if the groom's family has to go out and purchase things. So that night, my father told all the women, "If you would like to ask the groom's family for something, ask them tonight. Tomorrow we want to focus on the wedding, and nothing else." I felt protected by my father, knowing that he wanted everything to go well in the morning. The women stayed up working and singing songs the whole night, but my maid of honor and I went to sleep in my Grandmother's room so we would be well rested the next day for the wedding.

Chapter 4

The Wedding

Early on the morning of my wedding day, my mother crept into my room and woke me up. She said, "Lets pray together." I'll always treasure that quiet moment with her, seeking God in the stillness before the boisterous and joyful wedding that followed.

We had asked one couple to stay with Jon's parents to interpret and explain the ceremony to them as it went so that they would understand what was going on. In my culture, the bride gets dressed in her parent's bedroom. Then, when she is ready, she sits in there and waits for the groom's family to come and pick her up. Since Jon did not have many of his family there, the women from the church split up, and half of them stayed outside the house with Jon's parents, and half of them were in the house with me and my family. When it was time, the women outside started singing and the ones inside answered them in song. They continued back and forth, singing with excitement for the bride and groom.

When my mom finally opened the door to the room, they all surrounded me and my bridesmaids and sang and danced as we slowly made our way to the car. The women who had been with Jon's parents laid down their cloth wraps for me to walk on as a carpet all the way to the car. Jon waited at the bottom of the hill, because culturally the groom is not allowed to come to the house to pick up the bride. I was nervous, but the enthusiasm of everyone around me bolstered my confidence, and I was so excited that this day had finally come.

We drove down to the church in town and had the ceremony there. It was such a unique ceremony because we blended our two cultures and did some things the Kenyan way and some things the American way. We had a unity candle and Jon welcomed everyone to the wedding at the beginning of the ceremony, which were both unusual for a wedding in my culture. We also wrote and shared our own vows.

After the ceremony, the women surrounded us and sang and danced us into the reception. I loved it! It was my favorite part of the wedding. The reception was full of people from all over the community, because in my culture, a wedding is considered a community affair—no invitation is required. It was so packed that we couldn't get cake to the back of the room. People gave speeches and someone did an illustration with a tinsel garland. They tied the garland into a circle and had Jon and I hold it around us. Then they told us to invite our parents into the garland with us. When someone else stepped into the circle, the garland snapped. This was to illustrate that a marriage is between two people. If you invite someone else into your marriage, even a parent, the marriage could break. Most people gave us gifts of money, because they knew we were going back to the U.S., but we received a few memorable gifts as well. My dad and uncle both gave us cows, a friend gave us a goat, and several people gave us African baskets called *kiondos.*

My favorite childhood Sunday school teacher was there and I wanted her to have a special role in my wedding, so I asked her to be the cake cutter. I felt so blessed to have her come the whole way from her home to be part of the ceremony. Then the singing and dancing continued. The atmosphere was so carefree and happy. There were people everywhere and children all around.

After the reception, we borrowed a friend's car and started to drive away. Jon's mom, dad, sister, niece and some other friends were in the car in front of us. We had only gone about half a mile when our car stopped because it was out of gas. The other car didn't notice and kept driving. I was almost in tears, frustrated that something like this happened to us on our wedding day. Jon thought the whole situation was humorous, so his attitude helped to lighten the mood.

Eventually the other car realized we had stopped and came back to tow us to the gas station. The gas station ended up being close to where we had planned to spend the night, so we didn't end up wasting much time after all.

The next morning, we stopped by my parents' house to see the family. My mom was so glad to be able to see us before we left for our honeymoon. We visited for a little while and then left for Nairobi. After the long drive, we arrived at the place we were planning to stay, already tired. When we opened the door to our room, I saw the accommodations. There were two tiny, dingy looking single beds. I panicked. This was not how I had pictured my honeymoon. I looked at Jon and said, "I don't like it."

He said, "Don't worry. I'll see what I can do." So he went downstairs and talked to the management. When he told them that we were on our honeymoon, they gave us a cute little cottage away from all of the main rooms, with a bigger bed and a little more privacy. Once again, everything turned out fine.

In yet another honeymoon incident, Jon was pulled over and given a ticket by the police. However, the bill for the ticket was never sent, so we never had to pay it. Despite so many things seemingly going wrong, in each case, the outcome was positive.

After our honeymoon, we planned to stay for a few weeks and then go back to the U.S. Instead, it took me three months to get the FBI checks for my visa. The embassy suggested that Jon go back to the U.S. and have me follow once the paperwork was complete since it was unclear how long the process would take, but we were newlyweds and didn't want to be separated right away, so Jon stayed.

During that time, we moved in with my maid of honor. That allowed us some extra time with my family so that they could continue to get to know Jon and be a part of our lives before we moved back to the U.S. We never knew when the embassy would give us the go ahead, so we didn't make any plans. That gave us a lot of free time to ourselves. We enjoyed that time of forced leisure. Eventually, everything came through, so we bought our tickets, said our goodbyes, and moved to the U.S. for our first three years of marriage.

Chapter 5

Becoming Parents

In my culture, people usually have babies as soon as they get married. Jon and I waited for a year, so by the time I got pregnant, I was ready for a baby. We were renting a duplex and Jon's sister Jody lived in the apartment above us. She helped out on days when I felt too sick to do anything. For the first six months, I felt nauseated all day, but that didn't stop me from daydreaming about my baby. I would try to picture our new little one, wondering which of us he would resemble more.

As I approached my due date, I was increasingly anxious to meet my baby and be finished with the awkward and uncomfortable stage of pregnancy. But my due date came and went with no baby. A week later when Jon's parents came, having planned to help out with the baby, the baby still hadn't come. One night, the family sat together praying, and Jon's father said simply, "Lord, you know why we're here." At that moment, a giggle escaped from Jon's sister Jody. I couldn't keep myself from laughing in response, and before we knew it the entire family couldn't stop laughing. The laughter served as a welcome break from the mounting suspense of waiting for the baby.

When November 22nd rolled around two weeks after my due date, the doctor induced labor. Joshua came out healthy and screaming and Jon showed him to his grandparents, aunts, uncle and cousins on the way to get checked in the nursery. Finally, they brought him to me. I was amazed as he rooted and latched on the first time I nursed him. "Who taught you to do that?" I asked him, as I stroked his soft head, filled with wonder at this new life that we had anticipated for so long.

When it was finally time to come home from the hospital, my sister-in-law helped us load up all of the gifts and gear we had accumulated in our short stay. When we got to the house to unload, a blue wreath was hanging on the door, welcoming Joshua home. The visiting family lingered for a few days, and I was surrounded by the bustle of people pampering me and helping with the baby. His grandma walked with purpose everywhere she went, showing me how to support his neck, change his diapers, and give him a bath. I was surprised when she suggested going for a walk or to the store, when in my culture, mother and baby often stay sequestered in the house for months. Slowly I got back my strength and became comfortable with the routine of caring for my precious baby.

But eventually, people had to return to their own homes and routines. Even Jon and Jody had to go back to work, so I was left alone in our apartment to take care of Joshua. Little by little, I felt a darkness crawling into my chest and clutching my heart. We knew that we would be returning to Kenya before long, and we had really wanted to avoid accumulating unnecessary furniture and clutter, so we used the same worn and shaggy couch that the previous tenants had left. The dark wood paneling in the living room seemed to close in on me, and I began to feel lethargic all day, as if my limbs were as heavy as stone.

I would retreat to our single bedroom, where the bright paint, curtains and bedspread lifted my spirits. It was like a little refuge of color and light when I felt the depression start to gnaw at me. Joshua's crib was in the corner embellished by an adorable bumper, and I loved to watch him sleep.

But even there, I fell deeper into darkness. I cried for hours, for no reason at all. One night we were planning to go upstairs to Jody's apartment for dinner, but I was seized with another bout of weeping and couldn't stop. Jon patiently waited beside me, doing his best to comfort me and juggle the baby at the same time, but I still couldn't stop. "Just take the baby and go on up," I finally told him. "I'll come when I'm finished."

Eventually, the tears subsided. I wiped my eyes, took a deep breath to compose myself, and went up the stairs. When I sheepishly opened the door, instead of finding skepticism or pity, they just hugged me and said, "Come on in." Their gracious spirit was like salve on my instinctive shame and embarrassment.

After about two weeks of this, the world brightened again, as if a cloud had drifted away from the sun. I continued to gain back strength and energy, and felt more like myself again. One time when I was talking to my sister-in-law, she said that it was called postpartum depression, and that many women struggle with it. Little did I know what lay ahead.

We Africans like our babies to be nice and chubby. By the time Joshua was five months old, he was a chubby baby. He nursed for the first five months, and when I took him to the doctor he asked me what I was feeding him. I said I was just nursing him. He said, "You must have milk like an elephant!" I was able to educate some of my friends who didn't know the advantages of breastfeeding, because when they saw Josh, they couldn't believe how chubby he was, and asked what I was feeding him. Joshua was healthy and thriving, and all our family and friends doted on him.

Chapter 6

Back to Kenya

Jon and I had always wanted to go back to Kenya so that we could experience my culture. We contacted a few different missions agencies about serving in Kenya, but each time the plans fell through. Finally we talked to an indigenous church and they welcomed us to come.

When Joshua was about fifteen months old, we finally packed up and moved back to Kenya. We began ministering at a church in Juja, and felt content. We enjoyed the people and the ministry and settled into life. I felt light and happy being closer to my family again and living the life we felt called to. Growing up, I had always idolized our pastor's wife who taught my Sunday school class, and here I was, married to a pastor and organizing a thriving Sunday school ministry for the children. I was very satisfied.

When I found out that I was pregnant again, we were excited to add to our growing family. I looked forward to another baby and a sibling for Josh. But as the pregnancy wore on, I felt myself more and more frequently being dragged down by irrational feelings of fear and despair. The feelings overwhelmed me until I was sure I was going to die. I didn't want Joshua to grow up not knowing his mother, so one day I got out our tape recorder and started to read his favorite children's books into it. I wanted to preserve my voice so that if I died, he would still have a part of me. I didn't know what was going on or how to fight what was happening to me.

The pregnancy progressed without any complications, and to my surprise, I didn't get sick or injured, and my life was not threatened in any way. My sister was living with us, and as my due date approached, she helped take care of Joshua. I was planning to have the baby at Kijabe Hospital, which was several hours away, so when my labor pains started a few weeks before the due date, we left for Kijabe. I was admitted to the hospital when we arrived, and fell asleep there. When I woke up in the morning, the contractions had stopped. I tried walking around and keeping active to try to get the contractions to start again, but nothing worked.

My brother's girlfriend lived near the hospital, so we moved in with her for a couple of days, wanting to stay close. But when the contractions still didn't come back, we decided to go home. We spent the next week or so on high alert, but I didn't have any more contractions. The baby was due on Monday, so Friday, I said, "In two days, we are going to Kijabe, no matter what."

Jon raised his eyebrows, and said, "No discussion?"

I nodded my head firmly and said, "No discussion."

He smiled, and said, "Okay."

So on Sunday we packed up, went to Kijabe, and stayed at a motel near the hospital. That night I went to bed and I couldn't sleep well because I was so pregnant and uncomfortable. I tried to sleep anyway, knowing that I was due any day and needed rest. Around 2:00 AM I woke up with contractions and two hours later, we left for the hospital. Joseph was born around noon on Monday, right on his due date. He was a big handsome baby.

After he was born, I tried to get up to go to the bathroom, but I had lost some blood and stood up too quickly. Before I knew it I was dizzy and the room was getting dark. I called out for Jon and he caught me just before I fell. The doctor examined me, but they couldn't find any serious problem and just told me to rest. My brother brought Joshua to see his little brother. He couldn't stop staring at the little baby. He would watch him in awe, even though all he did was sleep and cry.

We only spent a few days in Kijabe and then we made the trip back home again. A couple of months later, a man from a neighboring town had died, so we took the baby with us and went to sit with the family in mourning. When we got back home, I began to feel the old darkness settle over me. Even with my sister living with us, I felt lonely at home with a toddler and a young baby, and I felt like I couldn't cope. I couldn't eat. I didn't have an appetite and when I tried to eat, food tasted like gravel.

With my first child, I couldn't stop crying, but with my second I couldn't stop my baby from crying. Since I wasn't eating, I wasn't producing enough milk and the baby was always hungry. I felt overwhelmed trying to take care of the kids because I didn't have any energy. I felt completely helpless.

Two of my friends came to visit me, and I explained what I was feeling to them. They listened and decided it was serious enough that they talked to Jon and suggested that he take me to the doctor. It hadn't occurred to me to go the doctor, because I didn't understand what I was feeling. There wasn't any particular part of me that was hurt or broken, but I felt sick.

When Jon and I got to the doctor, I was doubled over. I felt like I was only half conscious, and I laid my head on her desk. The doctor took one look at me and said to Jon, "I know what this is. We see this all the time with new mothers." She diagnosed me with postpartum depression, and gave me some medication to help me function. This began a journey of taking antidepressants which has continued to this day.

When we got home, one of the women had taken over the kitchen and cooked a fresh meal. When the food was ready, she set a place for me, held the baby, and told me to eat. She said, "I know you don't feel like eating right now, but just try to finish your food so you have some milk to nurse the baby." So she held the baby and talked to me while I ate. I fed Joshua, and then took my medicine, and it knocked me out right away. It made me too tired to feed the baby or even eat myself. Even three days later, when a couple came for counseling with Jon and me, I wasn't able to stay awake.

But in a week or two, the medicine began to take effect. I finally began to feel a little bit more like myself again. I was eating regularly again and the baby was easily satisfied. When I had been taking it for a couple months, I finally felt like I could handle my daily responsibilities. I felt like I had been healed, so I decided to stop taking the medicine.

Before long, I was struggling again. I would feel overwhelmed by simple tasks. I was too tired to work and sometimes too tired to even get out of bed. So I would start taking medication again, and repeat the cycle. I sought out healing anywhere I could. Sometimes I would read books and feel as though I had learned more and prepared myself to face anxiety and depression. I would say to myself, "Now I am prepared to deal with it. I don't need my medicine anymore." But as soon as I stopped the medicine, I would be mired down in the pit again, trying to climb my way out. I read every book I could get my hands on, went to every prayer meeting that was praying for sick people, I had the elders lay hands on me, I was anointed with oil, and was really actively searching for healing, but every time I stopped my medicine I would go back to struggling again.

At one point when the kids were little, I was having a very hard time coping with my symptoms. Jon ended up doing most of my chores and took care of the kids. One day I came out of the bedroom and saw Jon in the living room carrying the baby. He looked perplexed, with his hand on his head, as if trying to figure out how to juggle the baby and everything else he needed to do.

In my entire struggle with anxiety and depression, that was one of the most stressful moments. I thought, *I am supposed to be taking care of the children, and I'm not. I'm not helping and I'm not doing anything.* I began to sink deeper into despair, and began to feel worthless because I felt I wasn't contributing to the family. I thought, *I'm not being a good wife. I'm not being a good mother. All I do is lie around on the couch feeling depressed. They would be better off without me.*

Later, when I was in my room, I saw a long cloth wrap. I thought to myself, *If I hang that over something, I can end this right now.* But the thought was interrupted when I felt the Holy Spirit nudging me to call my doctor. I told her what I was thinking and feeling.

She said, "Where are you?"

I said, "I'm in my room."

She said, "Is there anyone there with you?"

I said, "My kids are in the living room."

Then she said, "Go sit in the living room with the kids. I'll be right over." So she closed up her office and came immediately.

I continued to struggle over the next several years, and the church rallied around us. Some of my good friends from church were prayer warriors, so I called some of those women together to pray with me. We prayed that I would be healed, and I stepped out in faith, stopping my medicine yet again. But again, I was forced to start taking it when my symptoms returned.

We noticed that I would have an especially bad attack every time we had a crusade planned where Jon needed to be out evangelizing. When I talked to another friend about this, she said, "Oh, I know what that's like. The Devil will do anything he can to keep your husband from focusing on his ministry."

What she said made sense, so I asked her, "What should I do about it?"

She said, "You need to start praying in advance, before the crusade even begins, so that Satan won't get you with your guard down." So that is what I did, and from then on, the attacks during crusades weren't as bad. That hasn't stopped even to this day. Sometimes when Jon has a ministry or a missions trip, or has to go somewhere, I have to go to the doctor. But we are more prepared than we used to be.

While we were living in Juja, our youngest, Elizabeth, was born. She was the prettiest baby girl I had ever seen. I was on antidepressants throughout my pregnancy and after she was born, so I didn't struggle with the same issues I had with the other two. I was in tune with her needs and was able to care for her myself, where I had had to rely on others with my first two.

When she was about three years old, we moved to Thika where Jon started doing leadership training. At the time, Jon was an overseer for thirteen churches with the African Christian Church (ACC). We began going with him to visit one or another of these churches each week, but I felt the need connect with one church, so the kids and I started to attend the mother church in Thika, and began ministering there.

Jon grew up in the Mennonite church, and I grew up in the Africa Inland Church, so neither of us had grown up in a very charismatic setting. I believe that God placed us at ACC, so that we could learn about spiritual warfare and how to pray against the enemy. During our time there, I really searched my heart to discern if my anxiety and depression was caused by some sin in my life. I came to feel assured that it was not a spiritual issue, but a *physical* one.

Chapter 7

Building a House

When we began to have issues with our landlady, we decided to build our own house. That house was our miracle house. Jon had received an inheritance from his parents, so we used that money to start the project. We hired a foreman, designed the house and started working. We spent a lot of time at the work site, and in the evenings, I would sometimes cook porridge for all the workers and bring it over, like my mother had always done when she had workers.

On the morning that they planned to pour the concrete slab, I was at our rented house when it started to rain. I knew that once you started pouring concrete for the slab, you had to finish the job right away. I prayed and asked the Lord to keep the rain from the site of the house, just three miles away. When I took porridge for the workers in the evening, they told me it had not rained there. God had answered my prayer!

But before long, the money we had set aside to build the house started to dwindle. We had decided not to take out any loans, so when the money was all used up, we knew we would have to stop building until we got more. The evening before we planned to halt the building, another miracle happened when some friends invited us over for a snack. After we had eaten together, they said, "We have some money for you, to help you build your house."

We couldn't believe it. God had provided for us in the exact moment of our need. The next day, instead of telling the foreman we had to halt the project, we took him to buy the needed supplies to keep building. Another of our friends took it upon himself to raise money to cover the cost of a wall, and little by little the money came together to continue building.

We had to be out of our rented house a few days before we were scheduled to go on furlough, so we moved our family and all of our furniture into the unfinished house, and lived with an unfinished floor until we left. We were in America for a couple of months, and then went back to Kenya and enjoyed living in our miracle house for two years.

Chapter 8

Victor, Not Victim

I struggled with anxiety and depression on and off throughout those years, and the longer I dealt with it, the more I learned about it. I began to come to a place of acceptance. I came to understand it as an illness rather than a curse or punishment. A special verse for me was Galatians 3:13: "Christ redeemed us from the curse of the law by becoming a curse for us, for it is written: 'Cursed is everyone who is hung on a tree.'" I still don't understand why God hasn't chosen to heal me, but I no longer feel that it is because of my lack of faith or because I am doing something wrong. Shortly before we moved to America in 2004, after living in Kenya for 13 years, I finally spoke openly about my anxiety and depression in front of our church. It was so freeing to share my struggle with them and to know that I didn't have to be ashamed of it or hide it.

It was hard to see God's purpose for my struggle in the beginning. I still don't understand it completely, but through walking this journey, I have grown closer to God. Since moving back to the U.S., I have continued to speak out about anxiety and depression. I started Freedom In Him Ministries, sharing my story and what I have learned with other women who are experiencing the same thing. I was surprised to find the stigma in the United States of America as well. I thought it would just be in Kenya. When I share about it, people walk up to me and whisper that they are also struggling with it, or are also on medication.

When I spoke at an institution one day, a man asked me to visit his wife afterwards. I went to her house that afternoon, and as soon as I looked in her face I could see that she was fighting with the same depression I had so often faced.

I sat with her for a while and she talked about how she was feeling, and ways that she tried to cope. She said she didn't want to take any medication because she was afraid of the kind of person she would become if she was on medication.

I said, "Do I look like I'm taking medication to you?"

She looked at me, and said, "No."

I said, "Well I am. The medication I take allows me to be *more* like my normal self so that I can be a good wife and mother." I said, "I may not be healed, but I am whole."

At that moment, the truth of those words struck me. I wasn't any less of a person because I struggled with the diseases of anxiety and depression. I finally felt released from the pressure of always feeling that I hadn't prayed hard enough or believed completely enough. God made me. He loves me even with anxiety and depression and I am whole.

My story isn't over. I still struggle with anxiety and depression, and I still pray for healing. I have chosen not to be a victim, but to walk in victory. God has redeemed my pain, so that I am able to stand in front of women and share my story to help others. Each time I speak, I hear from women who are suffering in silence because they are afraid of the stigma of mental illness. By speaking out, I am helping to break down that stigma. God is using my openness to bring wholeness to me by redeeming my pain to bring healing to others.

People who are afraid to share what they are struggling with hear my story and think, "Oh. So I'm not crazy. And I'm not alone." People who struggle with mental illness are no different than people who struggle with all kinds of other issues. We are all broken, and we live in a broken world. But we live our lives victoriously in spite of it.

Part 2:

Understanding Anxiety and Depression

Chapter 9

Anxiety

Coming to understand anxiety and depression as a physical disease rather than a personal flaw was the turning point in my journey to victory. Learning about these diseases can take away some of the enigma that makes them feel insurmountable.

Being diagnosed with Generalized Anxiety Disorder put a name to the feelings I had been struggling with, and allowed me to study the disease so that I could understand what was happening to me. Generalized Anxiety Disorder is a state of thinking in which an individual is always worried about something bad happening. The person lives with a sense of dread, and in most cases, it is unrealistic worrying. This makes life a constant state of worry and fear and dread.

To understand anxiety and depression we need to look at how God created our brains and how the brain works. The brain sends messages to all parts of the body. It communicates to the legs and feet when it is time to walk, and it also controls our heart beats and our emotions. These messages are sent through nerve cells called neurons which use chemicals called neurotransmitters to send messages to each other.

These brain chemicals—in varying amounts—are responsible for our emotional state. Sometimes an imbalance can be the root cause of anxiety. This condition can be passed on from one generation to the next. Other times, people struggle with anxiety because of traumatic experience they have gone through such as the death of a loved one or being involved in a car accident.

The symptoms of anxiety include sweaty palms, lack of focus on tasks, shaking, anger, insomnia, jumpiness, headaches and nausea. Some of these symptoms can lead to panic attacks, and disorders such as obsessive-compulsive disorders and phobias. Panic attacks are one of the most difficult symptoms of anxiety. Panic attacks are cruel; they come upon a person suddenly and are completely overwhelming. They can cause a feeling of great fear, sweating, and heart palpitations. All these factors can get in the way of the individual living everyday life as they should.

One of my biggest frustrations with Generalized Anxiety Disorder is that it happens subconsciously. Many times I don't realize I'm becoming anxious until it has already built up. For me, it feels like I work myself into a lather, and then once I realize what is going on, I need to take steps to calm myself down. I have learned to distinguish the symptoms and work with my mind before I hit the "boiling point" of anxiety. I don't always catch myself, but when I do, I can work with my mind.

I also struggled with fear of leaving the door unlocked at night. This was like being in a self made prison where I would go lie down then wake up check the door repeatedly until God finally delivered me from the obsession. I still check the door to make sure it is locked, but not more than once.

Panic attacks always took me by surprise, even after I had struggled on and off with anxiety and depression.

One time we were in Nairobi, and Jon dropped me off to do some shopping. I was just walking along when all of a sudden my heart started racing and I felt like I was going to fall over. I was sweaty and shaky, and I thought, *I must be dying!*

I walked into the nearest store and told the lady what I was feeling, and she graciously gave me a place to sit. After my heart had slowed down, she had one of her employees walk with me to meet Jon. I just wanted to stay home and never go outside my door, because I felt afraid that I would have another panic attack.

Telling someone else that you are having a panic attack can really help keep you grounded during the scary experience. It is always more bearable when I'm with someone I know and trust.

Chapter 10

Depression

Depression hurts! Many times I have wished that I had a broken foot or arm, or a sore I could show people so they would understand my pain. It hurts and it can drain energy and all desire to be alive. I remember feeling that I was the most horrible wife and mom. I started feeling useless and then the enemy started attacking my mind with suicidal thoughts. The other sad thing with depression is that it is not something you walk around telling everyone. Again, the enemy would take advantage and encourage me not to tell anyone about my suicidal thoughts.

Depression has many causes. It can be caused by traumatic events such as the death of a loved one, and sometimes other sicknesses can also cause depression.

Significant changes, even good changes, can come with a loss that can trigger depression as well. Some personalities are more prone to depression than others.

Just like anxiety, it can be passed on genetically. Mary L. Testa explains, "Depression happens when chemical messages aren't delivered correctly between brain cells, disrupting communication. Think of a telephone: if your phone has a weak signal, you may not hear the person on the other end. Their communication is muted or unclear" (www.marytestacounseling.com).

My friend Janice Martin, a nurse, wrote the following piece describing the chemical reactions of the brain.

> *In the beginning, God programmed man's brain cells to function in the exact manner needed for his body, soul and spirit to have balance and rhythm. Every cell knew it's exact job and performed it in complete harmony with all the other cells. When Adam and Eve sinned, death entered the nervous system as in all other body systems, and things ceased to flow smoothly. There was friction and chaos instead of perfect equilibrium.*

Many, many generations later, a descendent of Adam and Eve, by the name of Betty, was born into this world and her human genetic inheritance caused her to experience stress from time to time.

For the sake of this story, we will focus on a single synapse between 2 individual cells in Betty's brain but remember there are actually hundreds of thousands of cells and millions of synapses involved. Cell A's primary function is to stimulate Cell B whenever Betty feels the need to be more alert. Cell A sends neurotransmitters carrying the message, "wake up and pay attention across the synaptic cleft to Cell B and Betty is now able to stay awake. At night, Cell A is programmed to send less messages so Betty can sleep.

Then one day, Betty is upset over a threatened relationship that is extremely important to her sense of worth and well- being. Cell A receives the message that a crisis is taking place and sends frantic messages to Cell B to be ready for an emergency who in turn passes the message on to

Betty's heart which begins to beat faster and to her muscles which tense for action. Cell A keeps sending messages at bedtime and Betty is unable to fall asleep and she lays awake worrying all night.

After several nights of little sleep, Betty decides to take a sleeping pill. The sedative is able to block most of Cell A's neurotransmitters from being released so Betty calms down and sleeps. Cell B notices the decline in messengers and is concerned about the abnormal state of affairs. Cell B sends messages back to Cell A asking what's wrong and tries to help by building more neuroreceptors and equipping them to be extra efficient. Cell A keeps trying hard to do its job and finally sneaks some neurotransmitters out by building new, secret exits. Betty now notices that she has to take more sleeping medicine than before to fall asleep.

Eventually Betty's relationship crisis resolves itself and Betty decides to stop taking her sleeping pills. Cell A is now free to work and goes crazy making up for lost time. It fires up to an extreme degree making and releasing neurotransmitters and they come raging in hordes across the synapse to Cell B who still has the extra extremely efficient neuroreceptors in place to receive them. Cell B goes berserk and sends wild, unorganized messages to the rest of the body. Betty's heart races, her temperature rises, her muscles twitch and her thoughts race. You can imagine how much sleep Betty will be getting that night.

The same kind of cellular dynamics apply to non-substance addictions. Your brain is trained to think in certain patterns. If you have heard negative talk and criticism all during your childhood, the first time someone tells you that God made you and values you as a special, important, lovable person your brain will have difficulty processing the message. New synapses and connections have to be formed and old ones dissolved. Neurotransmitters and receptors have to make changes.

Janice takes a very complicated system and makes it easier to understand. I found it very helpful to understand what is going on in the brain and the chemicals involved. Learning what is happening has helped me not to feel crazy or fearful about what was going on in my brain. I am able to understand that I have some chemicals missing in my brain. Understanding this helps me to be okay to take medication to help with the chemicals that are in short supply.

Chapter 11

Seasonal Affective Disorder

Seasonal Affective Disorder, or S.A.D can be caused by a disruption of the body's internal clock due to the reduced amount of sunlight in the winter months. This disruption causes the body not to be in sync with sleeping and waking times. In the fall and winter, the amount of sunlight decreases, causing some people to experience S.A.D. A disruption of the chemicals melatonin and serotonin can also cause S.A.D. When the balance of melatonin is disrupted, sleep patterns can change and cause S.A.D. If the levels of serotonin drop, a person's mood is affected. Again the lack of enough sunlight may cause the drop of serotonin levels.

When I came to the U.S., I was diagnosed with S.A.D. When I was diagnosed with S.A.D, I said, I don't want to be S.A.D, I want to be H.A.P.P.Y! But the winters have been the toughest time for that because of the dark dreary days with no sunshine. Some of the symptoms of S.A.D include lack of energy, feeling sleepy, sluggish and slow, depression, and weight gain.

This has been a new struggle for me. I have learned to stay in places that have lots of light and make sure my walls are light. When it gets really bad, I have a light that I sit in front of to make up for the lack of sunlight. This is called *light therapy* and can be prescribed by a doctor. I also enjoy the snow because it makes everything nice and bright. I don't enjoy the cold, but I enjoy the light of the snow. I make sure to appreciate it and take in the beauty of it to help me fight S.A.D.

Chapter 12

Suicide

I used to wonder how Christians could commit suicide but now I know. As I struggled with these disorders I felt ashamed to share about it with anyone else, since that would be a sign of lack of faith. But when we share our stories, we can help others who are having the same struggles as we are.

If you ever have suicidal thoughts, it's important to tell somebody. The devil wants you to keep quiet about it, because it makes his job easier. His job is to steal, kill and destroy (John 10:10). The more he convinces you you're not worth anything, and the louder the voice becomes in your head, the harder it is to hear the voices of reason trying to speak into your life.

Speaking out about thoughts of suicide breaks their power. The enemy wants us to be afraid and keep it to ourselves so that we have to fight the battle alone. That's why some people are afraid to tell anyone what they're feeling. This reminds me of cockroaches. When the light is shined on them, they scatter. In the same way, if we tell others about our suicidal thoughts, we expose the enemy and his plans.

My pastor once told me that when we are feeling suicidal we rationalize that our friends and family would be better off without us. He explained that this is a lie, because suicide would cause them pain for the rest of their lives.

During a time when I struggled with suicidal thoughts, I prayed, "God, please help me distinguish between Your voice, the devil's voice and my own flesh." And over the years, I have learned to do that. The truth, which God speaks, overrides the devil's lies.

Recently I was struggling with suicidal thoughts again, and I thought, *I should tell somebody.* I spoke to Jon and my pastor about it, and they each prayed with me and they both asked me to promise them that if I heard that voice again, to call them right away.

Later I was driving alone when the voice returned. It rationalized, saying, "You're not *really* going to kill yourself. You just want attention." I recognized the devils attempt to sneak in, and I said, "I'm going to tell on you."

So I told God and Jon the thought had returned, and he prayed for me again.

Anther reason to speak up is that you are not alone. I like to keep that in perspective because the enemy of our souls would like for us to believe that we are the only ones struggling with either depression or anxiety or both so that he can isolate us and literally suck the life out of us to the point to death.

Chapter 13

Medication

The good news is that there are many forms of treatment that can help people cope with depression, including medications that can strengthen weak signals in the brain by raising the levels of certain chemicals, or by improving the neurons' ability to process signals. This ensures that the brain's vital messages are delivered—loud and clear.

The bad news is that it is not an exact science. The doctor can prescribe medication that does not work and it may take two or three weeks of pain to realize that the medication does not work for you. So once again, you try another medication for two or three weeks to see if it will help. This can be a very frustrating process, but for some people, it can mean the difference between being overcome by anxiety and depression, and being able to function as a "whole" person.

I have used medication for more than twenty years now, but I still don't want my trust to be in my medication. There was a time when I became obsessed with my medication. I always had to know that it was with me and how many pills I had before I felt secure enough to go anywhere. Even if Jon asked me to go for a walk around the block, I would take a pill along in case I needed it.

Then I realized that my medication had a major hold on me. I put a handful of the medication in my palm, looked at it, and declared, "My trust is not in the medication, but in the God who heals." Sometimes God shows up in person and heals someone. Sometimes He uses doctors and medicine to heal us instead. But even if I go to a doctor and take medicine, I have learned that my faith for the healing should always be in God. It is in God that I find wholeness in spite of sickness.

When people learn that I am taking medication to manage my anxiety and depression, I get many different reactions. Some people believe that I should stop taking the medication and simply pray for healing. But I know that most of those people would not tell someone with diabetes to stop taking their insulin. One time as we were travelling, I saw a billboard beside the road that said, "You'd never hear, 'Snap out of it, it's just Diabetes.' Depressionisreal.org." It's difficult for some people to recognize mental health issues as legitimate physical diseases. But anxiety and depression have as much to do with the physiology of the body as any other illness.

I would be the first person to say I wish I didn't need to take medication, but I know that I need the medication until the Lord chooses to heal me completely. I pray that if and when that day comes, God will give wisdom to my doctors to recognize that I am healed and no longer need the medication.

The Bible references both medicine and doctors in Jeremiah 8:22:

"Is there no balm in Gilead?
 Is there no physician there?
 Why then is there no healing
  for the wound of my people?"

The dictionary defines a balm as an agent that soothes, relieves, or heals. What better description of medicine? Another reference can be found in Ezekiel 47:12:

> " Fruit trees of all kinds will grow on both banks of the river. Their leaves will not wither, nor will their fruit fail. Every month they will bear, because the water from the sanctuary flows to them. Their fruit will serve for food and their leaves for healing."

Once again, it seems clear that the leaves for healing are used for medical purposes. Of course miraculous healing is possible, and that is what I hope for, but God obviously has a place for medication. He is the creator of the chemicals that are medicinal agents.

Chapter 14

Triggers

I've learned through my walk with anxiety and depression that certain things will trigger an attack. By learning what my triggers are and avoiding them, I can protect myself from some negative thoughts and feelings that can drag me down. Instead, I try to focus on positive things.

I was a fearful child and sometimes let my imagination run away with me. When my friends and I would sit around in school during recess, they would tell scary stories. They were completely made up stories about giants who would eat people, or about a man who lived in a crater. But even though I knew they were fake, they terrified me.

One time I was going to a little garden a mile away from the house to get greens for supper. I took a basket and started walking there. When I saw a man in front of me, I remembered the stories and my imagination went wild. I got so scared that I ran home another way. To get back, I had to cross a dam. My heart was already beating from running away from the man, and when I noticed a whirlpool in the middle of the pond, it terrified me. I had to make my way across anyway, to get home. Sometimes I think that I opened the door to fear by listening to scary stories and reading novels.

Since becoming aware of the affects of triggers on my anxiety and depression, I have begun making a conscious effort to avoid them. I don't watch gory movies, or even the news before going to bed. The news is normally very negative and it reports all the bad things that happen, both next door and all around the world. Instead, I focus on the fact that I made it through the day, and view each task I completed throughout the day as an accomplishment.

One time I heard a preacher on the radio speaking about the end times. I started to feel the anxiety building inside of me and decided, "I don't need to be listening to this right now." So I turned it off. That was not because I am not ready for Jesus' return, but because there are people that I love who I would like to see come to Jesus.

I try to avoid spending too much time with negative people, because they drag me down with them. If you have trouble staying away from some of your triggers, ask for help. Your friends and family can help shield you from some of your triggers.

Part 3

The Journey to Wholeness

Chapter 15

The Power of God's Love

As I've travelled this journey with anxiety and depression, I have learned that there are five specific tools that I can use to fight it. The first of these tools is God's love. I grew up in a very hierarchical society, and that shaped my view of God. I always thought of God as this big man sitting up in heaven, waiting to hit us upside the head. Through my journey with anxiety and depression, I am also learning about the God who loved us enough to send His Son to redeem us. I am learning about His unconditional love, and that there is never a time when God doesn't love us. The knowledge of God as a Redeemer and as the Divine Lover has brought me great comfort.

Throughout the scriptures, beginning in Genesis, we see God's promise for a redeemer of humankind. This is fulfilled in the New Testament when Jesus is born to buy us back from sin and death and set us free from the hands of the enemy.

Every girl is romantic at heart. We all dream of a knight in shining armor coming to sweep us off our feet. Many times in the process we get wounded; our hearts are broken and all we have to show for those relationships are ashes. We are captives to our great desire for love and we go looking for it in all the wrong places. We live in darkness not knowing what true love is. We mourn the fact that we have not experienced what we dreamed of as little girls. Many women give up and live a life of despair because they have been disappointed when they tried to find love. They are in a cage with a broken heart. God is the only one who can love us perfectly and He loves all of us.

> "How priceless is your unfailing love! Both high and low among men find refuge in the shadow of your wings" (Psalm 36:7).

God loves us perfectly because it is in His very nature. He cannot help but love us.

> "Whoever does not love does not know God, because God is love" (1 John 4:8).

> "And so we know and rely on the love God has for us. God is love. Whoever lives in love lives in God, and God in him" (1 John 4:16).

God loves us and He has included us in His family.

> "How great is the love the Father has lavished on us, that we should be called children of God! And that is what we are! The reason the world does not know us is that it did not know him" (1 John 3:1).

It is amazing that God did not wait for us to clean up our lives before He sent Jesus. The Bible says in John 3:16, "For God so loved the world that he gave his one and only Son, that whoever believes in him shall not perish but have eternal life." He sent Jesus to die for us even before we knew God. This was a great way to show His love.

> "But God demonstrates his own love for us in this: While we were still sinners, Christ died for us" (Romans 5:8).

Zephaniah 3:17 continues to show His love for us as He quiets us with singing:
> "The LORD your God is with you, he is mighty to save. He will take great delight in you, he will quiet you with his love, he will rejoice over you with singing" (Zephaniah 3:17).

Can you picture that in your mind? God taking *great* delight in us, quieting us down like a mother with a fussy baby, and rejoicing over us with singing. What great love He has shown to us. When we see His love and accept it without feeling like we need to do anything to earn it, then we enjoy freedom in His presence daily. Knowing God and experiencing His love comes from spending time with Him in scripture and prayer times. David

Benner (2004) writes in his book *The Gift of Being Yourself,* "Spending time with Jesus allows us to ground our God-knowing in the concrete events of a concrete life. But how do we actually do this? We do it by means of Spirit-guided meditation on the Gospels" (p. 37).

Notice, he wrote "meditating on scriptures!" There are too many people teaching on other kinds of meditation. Some are even inviting their audiences to empty their minds. This is a dangerous path which is marked by cultic beliefs that do not glorify God.

No human being can love us like God does I heard a preacher at church say, "If you ever look to anyone to love you in a way that only God can, you will always end up bleeding emotionally." Allow Him to love you. He wants a relationship with you. Benner (2004) writes, "What God longs for us to experience is intimate knowing that comes by means of an ongoing relationship" (p. 36). The creator of the universe wants a relationship with you. He is waiting, any time at any place, for you to sit with Him and enjoy His presence. Imagine that! In the Bible we see Jesus came to visit Mary and her sister Martha. Jesus was in their home to spend time with them, but Martha was so busy doing other good things and only Mary chose to sit at the feet of Jesus and learn from Him. That is how intimacy is expressed.

Allow Him to "hug" you, not because you deserve it or have done anything to earn it, but because He has done all that can ever be done to bring you back to the most beautiful and intimate relationship of all.

The dictionary definition of *redeem* is, "to buy back what was yours to start with." God is our Redeemer. Because of sin, the human race had been separated from God. God sent his own Son to come and die for our sins. He paid for us through His blood. The verses below show how much God values us and how He redeems us.

> "For your Maker is your husband—
> the LORD Almighty is his name—
> the Holy One of Israel is your Redeemer;
> he is called the God of all the earth.
> The LORD will call you back
> as if you were a wife deserted and distressed in spirit—

a wife who married young,
 only to be rejected," says your God.
'For a brief moment I abandoned you,
 but with deep compassion I will bring you back.
 In a surge of anger
 I hid my face from you for a moment,
but with everlasting kindness
 I will have compassion on you,'
 says the LORD your Redeemer" (Isaiah 54:5-8).

"I know that my Redeemer lives, and that in the end he will stand upon the earth" (Job 19:25).

"I am the LORD your God, who brought you out of Egypt so that you would no longer be slaves to the Egyptians; I broke the bars of your yoke and enabled you to walk with heads held high" (Leviticus 26:13).

God is so good to us. With mental health issues it is easy to think that God is punishing us or that He deserted us, and sometimes even that He does not care about us anymore. The truth is that even though He is Mighty,

Holy, Majestic, and the Commander of the heavenly host, God is *so* good to us. He has a gentle and compassionate side that He wants us to experience. When we hurt, He longs for us to come to Him for comfort and healing.

> "And he passed in front of Moses, proclaiming, 'The LORD, the LORD, the compassionate and gracious God, slow to anger, abounding in love and faithfulness'" (Exodus 34:6).

God proclaims who He really is. This verse brings me great comfort because it helps me to see a gentle, loving, compassionate God who is not angry with me. The Bible also shows He is gentle and when we are in pain, He desires to see us whole.

> "A bruised reed he will not break, and a smoldering wick he will not snuff out. In faithfulness he will bring forth justice" (Isaiah 42:3).

"A bruised reed he will not break, and a smoldering wick he will not snuff out, till he leads justice to victory" (Matthew 12:20).

Chapter 16

The Power of Forgiveness

The second of the tools to fight anxiety and depression is the forgiveness. When I have grudges or bitterness, the negative feelings pull me down. These negative feelings aren't healthy for anyone, but for someone who struggles with anxiety and depression, they can easily snowball and become debilitating. Keeping feelings of anger and bitterness inside brings us down and acts as a trigger for anxiety and depression. By refusing to give grudges and bitterness a foothold and by learning to forgive, I can shield myself from the negative feelings that may trigger an attack. God can use this forgiveness to heal us.

Many people who struggle with anxiety and depression are held captive by un-forgiveness. They may feel that forgiving someone is the same as saying that what they did was okay. Forgiveness doesn't mean condoning an action. It means having grace for that person, and letting go of the anger and hurt we feel. Forgiving sets us free. Henri Nouwen explains that God will provide us with the grace to forgive:

"We are all wounded people. Who wounds us? Often those whom we love and those who love us. When we feel rejected, abandoned, abused, manipulated, or violated, it is mostly by people very close to us: our parents, our friends, our spouses, our lovers, our children, our neighbors, our teachers, our pastors. Those who love us wound us too. That's the tragedy of our lives. This is what makes forgiveness from the heart so difficult. It is precisely our hearts that are wounded. We cry out, 'You, who I expected to be there for me, you have abandoned me. How can I ever forgive you for that?'

Forgiveness often seems impossible, but nothing is impossible for God. The God who lives within us will give us the grace to go beyond our wounded selves and say, 'In the Name of God you are forgiven.' Let's pray for that grace."

As a child, I had always dreamed of becoming a pastor's wife, just like my Sunday school teacher. I admired her beautiful and gentle spirit, and wanted nothing more than to be just like her when I grew up. So as I got older, I asked God to bring me a pastor to be my husband.

Long after I was out of that Sunday school class, I still held on to that prayer. One year, a group of pastors came to teach in our village, and my dad invited them over to our house. I made a connection with one of the young pastors in the group, and we started writing to each other. I thought the answer to my prayer had finally come.

We continued our long distance relationship, sending letters back and forth and I began to indulge my hopes for the future. But suddenly, the letters stopped. I wrote a few more times, and waited patiently, but never got a response.

My hope slowly faded, and hurt, confusion, and bitterness settled in its place. Whenever I met someone who shared that man's name, my stomach would tighten and I would feel anxious. Even after ten years had gone by, and I was happily married to Jon, I continued to feel a pang of anxiety when I heard his name. One night, I woke up and couldn't sleep. I felt the Lord ask me, "Who would you rather have as a husband? Jon, or that man?"

"Jon," I replied. There was no doubt in my mind.

"Then you need to forgive the other man," came the command.

I knew God was right, so I decided then and there to forgive the man for hurting me all those years ago. From then on, I stopped feeling the tightness in my stomach whenever I heard his name.

Several years later, Jon and I were at a pastor's conference. I was mingling in a crowd after the conference and Jon was at a booth selling books. Across the room, I noticed a man that looked familiar and when I saw his face, I realized it was the same pastor who had hurt me. It was the first time I had seen him since he had come to our village, and I nervously looked around for

Jon, unsure what to do. I was worried that the old feelings of bitterness would resurface, but they didn't. I found Jon and then went up to the man and introduced them to each other without any negative feelings towards him.

The story continued. Years later, when we were living in America, Joshua, our oldest son, asked me if he could have a friend from school over for the weekend. I agreed, and when he brought him home and introduced him to me, I realized he was the son of that same pastor. I joyfully fed and hosted him that weekend with no lingering anger or bitterness. It was only then that I was sure that I had completely forgiven the pastor.

From time to time when anxiety rises up for no apparent reason, I need to delve into my past to find unforgiveness. My parents were wonderful parents but they weren't perfect. In our culture it was common for parents to beat their children for misbehaving, and I found I still had emotional scars from my childhood.

For years, I would begin to feel anxious as soon as Jon left the house for work in the morning. I prayed, asking God to show me where these feelings were coming from. God reminded me that if I did something wrong when I was little, my mom would wait until my dad had left for work before spanking us. Somehow I had transferred the anxiety over my dad leaving each morning onto Jon leaving each morning.

I had to deliberately work through these feelings before I was able to forgive my parents and release them. In doing so, I not only freed them, but I freed myself, and came to a place of more wholeness.

Sometimes making a conscious effort to forgive someone isn't enough. Even if we make the decision to forgive, if we don't internalize it, sometimes it only goes surface deep. When we were living in Thika, Kenya, we only had one car. Jon used the car during the day, but he would bring it back in time for me to get to the Theological Education by Extension (TEE) class at the church that I taught on Monday nights. One day he was late. I had gathered everything I needed for my class, but Jon still hadn't arrived. I was starting to get frustrated but I decided to forgive him.

When he got home, I grabbed my things and rushed out the door. He said, "Let me explain why I was late."

I said, "Don't worry. I already forgave you," and rushed out the door to my class. When I got back that evening after teaching the class, he was waiting for me.

Again, he said, "Let me explain why I was late."

I said, "Like I said before, I already forgave you."

He looked at me skeptically and said, "Well, you forgot to tell your face."

Even though I had decided to forgive him, I was still upset, and he could tell. It wasn't enough to make the decision. I had to make sure I processed it and meant it.

Forgiveness is not always easy. On another occasion, someone verbally attacked my husband, berated him, and made all kinds of untrue accusations. He and my husband worked things out between themselves, but I couldn't let it go. Every time it came to mind, my chest would constrict and my hands would get sweaty, and all of the hurt and anger would boil to the surface. God said, "Here you are, being eaten up by anger and bitterness. That man is probably happily living his life, and doesn't even think about this anymore." I realized that I was only hurting myself, so I forgave him.

But even though I made that choice, I would still remember that fight from time to time and feel upset about it. One day I heard a preacher speak about blessing and praying for our enemies. I started to pray for God to bless the man that had attacked my husband. Slowly the anger started to fade, as I replaced it with blessing.

Unforgiveness is a trigger for my anxiety, and it can be a trigger for depression as well. I met a woman whose husband had left her. She was left as a single mother to care for their two children. She sank into depression and was sick often. Eventually she started medication to treat her depression. One day, she invited Jesus into her life. Soon after this, she heard the Holy Spirit asking her to forgive her husband, so she got on her knees and forgave him. That was the last time she ever needed any medication for depression, because her depression had been caused by the hurt, anger, and bitterness that she felt toward her husband.

It is important to search our hearts and our lives to see what could be causing our depression. If we really want to know, God can reveal it.

Sometimes I feel that God created marriage to keep us humble as a place for us to practice asking and extending forgiveness. One time Jon and I were counseling a couple who was having marital problems. When it was the wife's turn to speak, she spewed off a list of the things her husband had done wrong. Some of them were more than three years old. Holding on to that resentment, and refusing to forgive, was eating away at their relationship. She was a bitter woman,

Sometimes bitterness is not taken seriously. It seems like a small thing, but Ephesians 4:31 says, "Get rid of all bitterness, rage and anger, brawling and slander, along with every form of malice." This means that bitterness is sin and it is one of those that so easily entangles us, like the foxes that King Solomon refers to when he says, "Catch for us the foxes, the little foxes that ruin the vineyards, our vineyards that are in bloom" (Song of Songs 2:15).

In Matthew 18, Peter asks how many times we should forgive our brother. Jesus says, "Seventy times seven." If you are living with someone who keeps hurting you over and over, it's important to keep forgiving them. But it is also important to find a time to talk and express your feelings, as well as to set boundaries so that you don't keep getting hurt.

Sometimes, I find it helpful to write down the time, date and place when I forgive someone. That way, if the devil tries to haunt me with those feelings of hurt or anger, I can go back in my calendar and say, "I forgave that person on this day, at this time, and at this place. I choose to forgive, and I choose to bless."

When someone asks me for forgiveness face to face, I find it helpful to respond by saying, "I forgive you and I release you from any guilt or sense of obligation you have felt." That way, I am not brushing off what happened, but truly accepting their apology. I also find that hearing myself say it sticks in my mind, so that later, when the Devil tries to bring it up again, I can hear my own words echoing in my head, saying once again, "I release you."

Forgiveness is a two way street. When we say or do something that hurts someone else, we need to ask for forgiveness. More than just a simple platitude, we need to take responsibility for what we've done. It's important to frame our words carefully so that we repent of the specific thing we did that hurt someone else. I suggest that we ask for forgiveness by saying exactly what we did wrong. For example, "I am sorry that I yelled at you. Will you please forgive me?" In this way, we take ownership of what we did wrong and also clearly ask for forgiveness.

Growing up, I never heard adults say they were sorry, and when I became a mom, I had a really hard time asking my children for forgiveness. But I felt it was important to be an example to them, so I tried.

One day, when Elizabeth was five or six years old, I was having a bad day. Sometimes it helped me to clean and organize, and I wanted to be by myself, so I went in my room to work. When Elizabeth walked in and tried to get my attention, I snapped, "Just leave me alone!"

I saw tears in her eyes as she turned to leave the room and pulled the door shut behind her. I felt bad immediately and followed her. I found her sitting on her bed in her room, and I looked into her eyes and apologized. No sooner had I said the words, than she turned toward me, flung her arms around my neck and said, "I forgive you, Mommy."

It's so freeing to ask for forgiveness from children because they forgive so easily. That's how God wants us to be. He wants us to be quick to release grudges, and to forgive quickly and cheerfully. The story is told of a child who had done something wrong, and was spanked by his dad. When it was time to eat, he came to the table with the rest of the family, but his dad told him to go sit in the corner by himself. His dad proceeded to say grace. After they said Amen, they heard a small voice coming from the corner, saying, "Lord, I thank you for preparing a table before me in the presence of my enemies." That is how he felt, because he had been disciplined but not forgiven. This is not a book on parenting, but I encourage all parents to model forgiveness to their children.

Sometimes it is hard to go and ask for forgiveness, because we don't want to look bad or hurt our pride. When Jon and I were ministering with some friends at a leadership conference, one of the leaders came up to me and asked if I would serve communion with him. He told me to pray about it, but back in my room, as I prayed, the

Lord reminded me that I had a grudge against this leader. Not wanting to have a confrontation, I prayed, "Lord, I forgive him and release him, but please don't make me ask him for forgiveness."

But I felt the Holy Spirit convict me and the Lord said, "Go talk to him."

I was embarrassed because now my grudge seemed petty and small, and I would have to reveal it to him in order to ask for his forgiveness. The short distance from my room to the conference room stretched on, as I dreaded the ordeal before me. When I got into the conference room, I walked up to him and said, "May I talk to you?"

We walked over to a corner, and in a low voice, I told him about my grudge and asked him for forgiveness. He graciously listened and took what I said seriously so that I didn't feel silly or frivolous. I felt so relieved to have a restored relationship with him, and was able to serve communion with him with a clear conscience.

Sometimes the hardest person to forgive is yourself. Even after asking for forgiveness, we continue to feel guilty about what we've done. In these situations, it's important to ask God for wisdom to know the difference between conviction and condemnation. The Lord convicts us when we do something wrong, in order to redirect us to redemption. Satan condemns us by trying to make us a slave to the guilt and shame we feel when we do something wrong, even after we have already been forgiven. Accepting God's forgiveness sets us free.

For those who struggle emotionally, there is great freedom from negative emotions when we forgive. In his book, *The Heart of Christian Leadership*, Jon Byler (2006) writes, "Forgiveness will set you free from negative emotion... Unforgivness takes a heavy toll emotionally, producing anger, resentment and bitterness. When you forgive, this burden is rolled off your shoulders, releasing the tension felt in your body. Many people cry during the process of forgiveness, as the pain and struggle are released" (p. 145).

It is true that un-forgiveness can keep us in bondage. In her book, *Lord, I Want To Be Whole*, Stormie Omartian encourages forgiveness. She writes, "Without forgiveness, we cannot release the past. Don't let unforgiveness keep you from the healing, joy, and restoration God has for you" (Omartian, 2001, p. 26).

Forgiveness, the Way to Freedom
Henri Nouwen

To forgive another person from the heart is an act of liberation. We set that person free from the negative bonds that exist between us. We say, "I no longer hold your offense against you" But there is more. We also free ourselves from the burden of being the "offended one." As long as we do not forgive those who have wounded us, we carry them with us or, worse, pull them as a heavy load. The great temptation is to cling in anger to our enemies and then define ourselves as being offended and wounded by them. Forgiveness, therefore, liberates not only the other but also ourselves. It is the way to the freedom of the children of God.

Chapter 17

The Power of Praise

The third tool to fight anxiety and depression is praise. I have found that praise is one thing that brings a lot of victory, no matter what I am struggling with. When I focus on praising God, I take the focus off of my feelings of anxiety or feelings of depression. Refocusing and looking to the Lord gives Him the glory and lifts my spirit.

> "Through Jesus, therefore, let us continually offer to God a sacrifice of praise—the fruit of lips that confess his name" (Hebrews 13:15).

Using Hebrews 13:15 as a guide, when I go throughout my day, I try to pay attention to what God is doing, and give Him the praise. When I teach somewhere, if someone approaches me afterwards and thanks me, or compliments me, I first praise the Lord, and then I say thank you. God created us to praise and worship Him. We will be praising and worshiping for eternity in Heaven, and our praise and worship here is just a shadow of what's to come.

Some people who struggle with mental health issues can tell when an attack is coming, or know that certain times of year are particularly difficult. There is victory in praising God when we are anticipating an attack, or when we are already down in the dumps. The dark winter months are hard for me, but I love Christmas music. Playing Christmas music and singing along lifts my spirits and helps me get through the dreary winter.

Throughout the year when I'm feeling low and tired, I turn on some Christian music and dance and sing along. It changes the environment of the entire house. A place that seemed depressing and dark becomes cheerful and lively. Even my family can feel the difference in the environment. When Paul and Silas sang in prison, an earthquake released their chains as well as the chains of those around them. When I sing and dance for the Lord, the chains of my depression fall away and I am free.

We can also praise God after we have come through a valley or a dark day. Even if we don't feel victorious, there is victory in praising God and doing what He created us to do.

I am continually learning about the power of praising God and giving Him the glory. One day, when Joe was on a YES team with Eastern Mennonite Missions, we had been anxiously waiting to hear from him. Just as I was about to run out the door to an appointment, he called. Since I was already running late, I only talked to him for a few brief moments. I left the house with tears in my eyes, disappointed because I had missed my chance to talk to him. I felt like a terrible mom and I missed hearing my son's voice.

Three hours later, I was home after my appointment, and Joe called again. It did my momma-heart good to be able to sit for fifteen minutes talking to my son. When we had finished talking, I thought, *God did something really special for me. He arranged it so that I could talk to my son again, since I wasn't able to the first time.*

When we met for a prayer meeting that evening, I said, "Look what God did for me," and I shared my story. It's easy to overlook the blessings that He puts in our life, and write them off as coincidences. But we should never forget that God likes to make us smile.

I am also reminded of my blessings when I hear about the trials that others face. When I hear a story of a woman with an abusive husband, I thank God for my loving and supportive husband. When I hear about people whose children have walked away from the Lord, I thank God that my children are following Him. When I hear about people who are starving, I thank God for the abundance of food that we have all around us. And I pray for each person in these situations that they will experience God's goodness as He restores and redeems.

There are great examples of the power of praise in scripture. I have already mentioned Paul and Silas. They were in the middle of great pain: they had been beaten up and they were chained to stocks that made their backs hurt, but in the middle of all that, they sang praises to God. God sent an earthquake and their chains fell off.

This reminds me to praise when I am in the middle of a battle.

King Jehoshaphat also mobilized his people to praise God as they were going to battle. Instead of having the army lead the way, he had the choir in front, and once again God moved on behalf of His people and defeated their enemies. This reminds me to praise before the battle.

Nehemiah reminds me to praise after the battle. He had come to Jerusalem to re-build the wall of the city. He organized the people and as they started working, their enemies started opposing them. God gave them victory and they finished the wall. To celebrate what God had done, Nehemiah had the choir stand on the wall and praise God.

The Psalmist is so full of praise to God, and sometimes he amazes me when he praises after a lament. He usually starts off expressing his pain and ends with praise to God. There are so many Psalms of lament that end in praise. Some examples are Psalms 7, 56, 57.

"For the director of music. A psalm of David.
How long, LORD? Will you forget me forever?
How long will you hide your face from me?
How long must I wrestle with my thoughts
and day after day have sorrow in my heart?
How long will my enemy triumph over me?
Look on me and answer, LORD my God.
Give light to my eyes, or I will sleep in death,
and my enemy will say, "I have overcome him,"
and my foes will rejoice when I fall.
But I trust in your unfailing love;
my heart rejoices in your salvation.
I will sing the LORD's praise,
for he has been good to me" (Psalm 13).

Chapter 18

The Power of the Word

The fourth tool to fight anxiety and depression is the Word. Understanding the physical aspects of anxiety and depression can release us from guilt and confusion. In the same way, understanding how the Bible speaks to these issues can empower us to move toward victorious living.

In Psalms 42 and 43, King David repeatedly laments, "Why, my soul, are you downcast? Why so disturbed within me? Put your hope in God, for I will yet praise him, my Savior and my God." It is clear that David, a man after God's own heart, also struggled with depression. It's encouraging to know that despite our struggle with depression, we can be a person after God's own heart and live victoriously.

Romans 12:2 tells us that we can test and prove what God's will is.

> "Do not conform any longer to the pattern of this world, but be transformed by the renewing of your mind. Then you will be able to test and approve what God's will is—his good, pleasing and perfect will" (Romans 12:2).

When we have doubts or feel worthless, we need to seek out God's truth. We can replace the guilt and shame with the promises He makes in His word. The truth we find in God's Word should affect our daily lives, and we can use it to battle against the enemy.

The Bible is full of God's life-giving promises. The following verses have promises that have been very meaningful to me.

> "I will not die but live, and will proclaim what the LORD has done" (Psalm 118:17).

When my mind feels overwhelmed, or during a panic attack if I feel like I am going to die, I remember and quote this scripture. Declaring the truth of scripture helps my mind refocus.

Another verse that helps me is when God speaks to Joshua and declares that He will never leave him nor forsake him: "No one will be able to stand up against you all the days of your life. As I was with Moses, so I will be with you; I will never leave you nor forsake you" (Joshua 1:5). This scripture reminds me that I am *never* alone. God is always close to me. He loves me and He cares about me.

Another scripture that ministers to me is Isaiah 41:10, which says, "So do not fear, for I am with you; do not be dismayed, for I am your God. I will strengthen you and help you; I will uphold you with my righteous right hand." God is inviting us not to fear for He has a strong, Holy right hand with which He will uphold us. What a great promise! What a life giving promise! We do not have to keep on striving and fighting with fear. God will hold us up! Isaiah 43 is also a great inspiration to me.

"But now, this is what the LORD says—
he who created you, Jacob,

he who formed you, Israel:
"Fear not, for I have redeemed you;
 I have summoned you by name; you are mine.
When you pass through the waters,
 I will be with you;
and when you pass through the rivers,
 they will not sweep over you.
When you walk through the fire,
 you will not be burned;
 the flames will not set you ablaze.
For I am the LORD your God,
 the Holy One of Israel, your Savior;
I give Egypt for your ransom,
 Cush and Seba in your stead.
Since you are precious and honored in my sight,
 and because I love you,
I will give men in exchange for you,
 and people in exchange for your life.
Do not be afraid, for I am with you;
 I will bring your children from the east
 and gather you from the west"(Isaiah 43:1-5).

These verses remind me that God created me and formed me in my mother's womb, so He knows me better than anyone else. He gives me a direct command to not be afraid because He has paid a great price to buy me back from sin and death. I rejoice in knowing He knows me by my name. That makes our relationship more intimate.

He makes the amazing statement that I am *His*. I belong to God, so even when I am struggling I have a Father who is on my side—a Father who claims me as His own.

The passage continues, reminding me that since I am in a fallen world, there will definitely be times that I will walk through fire; times that I will feel like I am drowning. But I need to remember that because He is my God and Savior, the rivers will not sweep over me nor the fires set me ablaze.

He continues to build me up by declaring that I am precious in His sight, and He loves me. Those are priceless words, especially when I consider who is speaking them. The God of the universe says He loves me. When God Himself declares that He loves me, I get more energy to keep living. When anxiety and depression feel like they have me by the throat all I need to do is remember that God will not allow them to destroy me. He also encourages me to not be afraid for He is with me. Hallelujah! What a great and mighty God!

John 17:17 says, "Sanctify them by the truth; your word is truth." The word of God can be used to sanctify the soul and mind. So when we take God's word as truth, we can apply it to our minds and experience victory. Because of the power of the Holy Spirit, who is the author of God's word, it becomes truth that will set captives free from the lies of the enemy. The Bible points out that he cannot tell the truth, for lies are his native tongue:

> "You belong to your father, the devil, and you want to carry out your father's desire. He was a murderer from the beginning, not holding to the truth, for there is no truth in him. When he lies, he speaks his native language, for he is a liar and the father of lies" (John 8:44).

Those who struggle with mental disorders are very vulnerable to the enemy's lies and since our brains are not functioning like they should be, we can easily be attacked through lies and believe them. The word of God will bring truth to our minds which will result in wholeness. The word of God is also described as a double edged sword.

> "Take the helmet of salvation and the sword of the Spirit, which is the word of God" (Ephesians 6:17).

> "For the word of God is living and active. Sharper than any double-edged sword, it penetrates even to dividing soul and spirit, joints and marrow; it judges the thoughts and attitudes of the heart" (Hebrews 4:12).

A sword is used in battle, both for self defense and to assault the enemy. Adam Clarke (1931) makes an interesting observation of the word being a double-edged sword:

"The law, and the word of God in general, is repeatedly compared to a two-edged sword among the Jewish writers, the sword with the two mouths. By this sword the man himself lives, and by it he destroys his enemies. This is implied in its two edges" (Power Bible, 1999-2005).

Here we see that the word gives us life as food for our souls, and yet at the same time it is used to destroy the enemy. If you do not stand your ground by wearing the full armor of God, which includes a sword, he is going to be dancing all over you and making your life miserable. You have a mighty weapon in your hand. Commit it to memory so you can recall it when you need to fight for your mind.

Some people do not like the language of fighting, and I wish we had another term that was friendlier but we are truly in a battle and we cannot sign up as conscientious objectors. We have to fight!

"As the heavens are higher than the earth,
so are my ways higher than your ways

and my thoughts than your thoughts.
As the rain and the snow
 come down from heaven,
and do not return to it
 without watering the earth
and making it bud and flourish,
 so that it yields seed for the sower
and bread for the eater,
 so is my word that goes out from my mouth:
 It will not return to me empty,
but will accomplish what I desire
 and achieve the purpose for which I sent it" (Isaiah 55:9-11).

When we are struggling emotionally, as we speak God's word and apply it to our various situations, victory is sure, for God's word is powerful. In Matthew 8, we find Jesus talking to a centurion. This man had come to Jesus asking for his servant's healing. "Then Jesus said to the centurion, 'Go! It will be done just as you believed it would.' And his servant was healed at that very hour" (Matthew 8:13). This man knew that he did not have to bring his servant to Jesus. All that was needed was for the master to speak His word and the servant would be healed.

Another Old Testament example of God's word going forth and not returning void is found in 2 Kings.

> "Before Isaiah had left the middle court, the word of the LORD came to him: 'Go back and tell Hezekiah, the leader of my people, "This is what the LORD, the God of your father David, says: I have heard your prayer and seen your tears; I will heal you. On the third day from now you will go up to the temple of the LORD" (2 Kings 20:4-5).

Once again God sends His word and it brings healing. The same God who spoke to both Isaiah and the Centurion is still speaking healing and wholeness to His people, and we need to grasp the truth and walk in it.

> "For the word of God is living and active. Sharper than any double-edged sword, it penetrates even to dividing soul and spirit, joints and marrow; it judges

the thoughts and attitudes of the heart" (Hebrews 4:12).

God's word is not a dead letter. It was written through His Spirit and He continues to minister through the written word to us. The word is sharp and it can be applied into every area of our lives. If we think that there are areas that are hidden from God and intentionally try to keep those areas closed, hoping that God will not point them out, we are missing the point. The word of God can go into the deepest parts of our inner being and bring conviction, encouragement, healing and wholeness.

The word calls us to align our thoughts and attitudes with His. If we allow God's word to pierce into those secret places and judge our thoughts, then we will gain victory in the battle for our minds. As we read the Word and meditate on it, allowing the same Holy Spirit who wrote it to apply it to our minds, when we struggle with negative, fearful, unwholesome, or sinful thoughts, the Word will bring truth into those areas.

Look at this example of a mighty prophet who gets caught up in a battle for his mind:

"There he went into a cave and spent the night. And the word of the LORD came to him: 'What are you doing here, Elijah?'

He replied, 'I have been very zealous for the LORD God Almighty. The Israelites have rejected your covenant, broken down your altars, and put your prophets to death with the sword. I am the only one left, and now they are trying to kill me too'" (1 Kings 19:9-10).

Elijah's thoughts are full of fear. He is anxious and depressed, so he goes into hiding and has a pity party. God does not just sit in heaven watching him but shows up and speaks to him.

God sends His word to Elijah and instructs him to go to the entrance of the cave and Elijah gets a lesson on recognizing the voice of God. After the lesson God tells Elijah that he is not the only prophet alive but that there were seven thousand others who had not bowed to Baal. This gives Elijah confidence to step out of the cave and to realize that the enemy was attacking his mind with fear and lies that he was the only prophet left. God sent the exact words Elijah needed to hear to gain back his confidence in the midst of his struggle. In the same way He has given us His word so we can be victorious in our own struggles.

> "Let the prophet who has a dream tell his dream, but let the one who has my word speak it faithfully. For what has straw to do with grain?" declares the LORD. "Is not my word like fire," declares the LORD, "and like a hammer that breaks a rock in pieces" (Jeremiah 23:28-29).

The power of God's word is appropriately described in the above passage. It is like a fire which burns away the lies we believe about ourselves and others; a fire that purifies our thoughts and attitudes so we have a godly and positive outlook on life. It is also like a hammer that can crush those areas where we have allowed unbelief to dwell for so long that it takes a mighty force to bring truth.

In his sermon *Don't stop swinging that hammer,* Dan Downey (2004) says about the word of God, "The Word of God is a fire that purges and melts away all impurities, just as fire purifies precious metal, leaving only that which is treasured. It is also a hammer that is able to crush even the most resistant, stubborn circumstances, even those that seem so hard that they could never be removed. The Word of God is what it is - the very Word of God! The question is not in the ability of the Word, it is in our perception of it" (www.savedhealed.com).

Clarkes's commentary on this verse gives the following picture of God's word as both fire and hammer.

"There may be an allusion to the practice in some mining countries, of roasting stones containing ore, before they are subjected to the hammer, in order to pulverize them. In Cornwall I have seen them roast the tin stones in the fire, before they placed them under the action of the hammers in the stamp mill. The fire separated the arsenic from the ore, and then they were easily reduced to powder by the hammers of the mill; afterwards, washing the mass with water, the grains of tin sank to the bottom, while the lighter parts went off with the water, and thus the metal was procured clean and pure. If this be the allusion, it is very appropriate" (Power Bible, 1999-2005).

Chapter 19

The Power of Words

"The tongue has the power of life and death, and those who love it will eat its fruit" (Proverbs 18:21).

We have looked at the power of God's word, but what about our own words? This is the fifth tool to fight anxiety and depression. Do they have any effect on how we feel or how we see ourselves? There is power in the words we say to and about ourselves and the words we hear from others. The above passage clearly shows that your words can either bring life or death to you or to those around you. In Matthew 9:20, we find a woman who had suffered for many years. She finally hears about Jesus and the Bible says, "She said to herself, 'If I only touch His cloak, I will be healed" (Matthew 9:21). Her words reflected her desire for wholeness and she declared that she would receive healing by touching His garment. She did what she said, and she was healed. How have you been talking to yourself? What are you saying about yourself? Are you declaring defeat or victory? Are you declaring the truth of how God sees you, or the lies you have come to believe about yourself? Yes, you have a choice in winning this battle through the words you speak about yourself.

If you have a tendency to be negative about yourself and to repeat negative things you have heard about yourself from others, then you will stay in a place of darkness. Sometimes as we are growing up, people say negative things about us, and if we believe them, we keep repeating them in our minds and this keeps us in a place of defeat. There are people whose parents told them they would not amount to much, so in response they have become workaholics. They can be very successful people in whatever they do, but because of those voices from the past, they can never see the success, and they continue to be slaves to past voices. But the Word of God overrides even the things that other people have said over us. Take a break and do an inventory of all the things you are doing and the success that you have had, and focus on that, rather than on failure.

Many times, I felt cared for and uplifted by the dedication and prayers of the people of the church, but sometimes the prayers struck a nerve. One time when a group of people got together to pray, I didn't feel well enough to come, so I stayed home. Jon went, and when he came back, he said the person who was praying had quoted 1 Corinthians 14:11, saying, "God is not a God of disorder, so we are going to believe in order, and pray for order." I was grateful that people were trying to build up my faith, but I began to feel that it wasn't fair. I thought to myself, *Is that what I am struggling with? Disorder? Does that mean I'm doing something wrong? Does that mean God is unhappy with me or has rejected me?* I wondered if I needed to be trying harder, or praying harder.

When someone is diagnosed with another disease, people expect them to take their medicine. But even though I had been diagnosed with anxiety and depression,

I felt constant pressure to get better and get off of my medication.

I have learned to listen to my body, so that I know what I need to continue to function as a wife and a mother. Taking medication can bring me to a place of wholeness. It is important to respond to what our body is telling us, rather than to the pressure from ourselves or others to be healed without medication.

Chapter 20

The Power of Prayer

The last tool we can use against anxiety and depression is prayer. There is such a blessing in coming to the Lord and bringing our pain and our frustrations before Him. The Psalmists didn't mince words in telling God how they felt. Sometimes their language even makes *me* uncomfortable, but it doesn't offend God to hear the truth of how we are feeling. He already knows it anyway.

For healing to happen, there has to be a lot of lamenting prayers. When I come to God with an open heart, and tell Him what I'm feeling rather than reciting some canned phrases over and over, I connect with Him on a much deeper level. I recently took a class on prayer and we looked at Psalmists' laments where they opened up their hearts, asked God questions and just told God exactly how they felt.

Here are some examples of laments:

"Why, O LORD, do you reject me and hide your face from me?" (Psalm 88:14).

"My God, my God, why have you forsaken me? Why are you so far from saving me, so far from the words of my groaning?" (Psalms 22:1).

"I say to God my Rock, 'Why have you forgotten me? Why must I go about mourning, oppressed by the enemy?'" (Psalms 42.9).

"Awake, O Lord! Why do you sleep? Rouse yourself! Do not reject us forever. Why do you hide your face and forget our misery and oppression?" (Psalms 44:23-24).

After reading some of these laments in my class, we were assigned to write a lament. I thought there was no way I could do that, because the laments sounded so harsh towards God, but the leader encouraged me to write one and I did. I wrote Him a lament about my struggle with anxiety and depression and it gave me the freedom to talk to God more openly.

My Lament
By Loice Byler

Dear Jesus,

Thank You for inviting me to be honest with You for it is only then that You'll be honest with me!

Lord, I struggle with anxiety and depression. It hurts so bad. It takes me to a place where I feel that even You have abandoned me. I cry out to You and You seem so far away. I am in pain yet Jehovah Rapha seems so far away. Why do You allow this in my life? What do You or anyone else gain from the pain?

It is unfair to continue to struggle when I gave You my all. Lord, I searched my life for sin and remain in the place of repentance before You. Yet that does not seem to satisfy You. Lord, sometimes it feels like I am in hell. Why do You allow me to hurt so bad? I know You as a healer.

Where's Your healing power? Why do You not manifest it in my life?

Lord, this sickness is so expensive. Why do You allow us to spend money on something that does not profit anyone?

When I am in deep pain, my husband hurts and struggles alongside me. My children feel fearful and helpless. Why do You bring pain to them? My mother worries. Why do You bring pain to her? This sickness affects so many people in my life. What do I gain from my pain?

My enemy arises to torment me. My enemy attacks, and keeps me in bed for days. Why do You allow me to waste so much time that I would have used to minister to others?

In the plans of darkness where is Your glory? In the times of pain where is Your healing hand? And at times of an attack where is Your protection?

Lord, I hurt when people see me and I can see it on their faces that they are afraid of me and they would rather not come close to me. At those times I feel alone, misunderstood, and stigmatized. Why should people treat me like an outcast? Lord that hurts so bad. Where are You at these times? Why do You add pain over pain?

You put my brain together in my mother's womb. Are You not the God with whom nothing is impossible? Why don't You create the chemicals in my brain one more time?

I see this sickness moving from generation to generation. If it was sin that brought it along, are You not the God who forgives? If it was a curse, are You not the God who became a curse for me?

I see Your Majesty in creation, majestic mountains, and beauty all over. Your word tells me that I am more important than the wildflowers, and more important than the birds. Would You prove that I am more important than they are by providing healing for me?

Father, I ask these questions and make requests because You want me to be honest with You. I thank You for the place of wholeness You have brought me to and I look forward to complete healing which only You can bring.

I sure felt heard by the Lord and comforted by Him. God doesn't only want to hear our prayers. He wants us to listen for His response as well. It's in the listening times that healing happens. God speaks truth and life. He has a Rhema word for each person, and they are all equally important. Prayer is about talking *with* God, not *to* God.

I find I often imagine God's voice, thundering down from heaven in King James English, but when I was struggling with my feelings one day, it wasn't like that. I was trying to do the dishes, but I just stood at the sink with tears streaming down my face. Suddenly I felt God's presence, and heard Him say, "It's going to be okay." There was no flowery language or claps of lightning, but He spoke the words my heart needed to hear, and within ten minutes I felt much better.

In Kenya, I was blessed to have a psychiatrist who prayed with me. She took time off of work once a week and came over to my house. I would set aside the homeschooling and housework, and for an hour we would pray together. When we moved to the U.S., I didn't want to give that up. I prayed that I would find a

Christian doctor that would pray with me, just as my psychiatrist in Kenya had.

We called around to a few doctor's offices and asked, "Do you know if the doctor is a Christian?" Eventually, I asked a friend of Jon's, and she suggested a doctor near us, so we set up an appointment to meet him. He was the answer to our prayer. He had just recently come back from serving as a missionary in Russia, and was readjusting to life in the U.S., like we were. So I began to see him, and he prayed with me. One time when I was sick, he called and said, "I was just calling to check in on you, and I want you to know that I'm praying for you." I felt comfortable knowing that he kept me in prayer.

Several months later, my meds were not working well. I called my pastor to let him know that I needed his prayers. When I told him that I was feeling overwhelmed, he said, "There's a psychiatrist who I'd like you to meet, but I'm not sure how to get in touch with him." That same evening, a friend called to see how I was doing. He mentioned the same psychiatrist by name, and said that he worked with him. I couldn't believe it when he mentioned the same exact man. Our friend arranged for me to meet with him the next day. Later, the psychiatrist came over to our house and anointed me with oil, gave me communion, and prayed over my medication. I feel more comfortable taking my medication knowing that my doctors are praying for me, and trusting in God.

Chapter 21

Encouragers

One very helpful thing you can do to support people with anxiety and depression is to encourage them. Pray for the person and let the person hear you praying. Encourage the person to get out of bed, comb their hair, hop in the shower, and put on clean clothes. This will make them feel better about themselves. You can do this lovingly without being pushy. If they don't want to, let it go and try again another time. Take their pain seriously, and consider it as a ministry that God will reward you for.

Also encourage those who are supporting people with anxiety and depression. Jon has been my biggest support during everything. He prays with me and encourages me. One night, we went to bed as usual and I fell right to sleep. Then I woke up around midnight and couldn't fall back to sleep. I woke Jon and asked if he would pray with me. He stayed up with me, praying and singing worship songs. I don't know what I would have done if I didn't have Jon for a husband. He is so supportive. He stays home with me when I need him to, and never complains. One time I was really struggling with driving, but I needed to get to work. He was going the opposite way, but he drove in front of me the whole way to work so I could follow him, and then turned around and went the other way to his own job.

Sometimes Jon will pick up on things that I don't even notice myself. If I am not sleeping well, or am starting to feel low, he points it out to me before I recognize it myself. He keeps a spreadsheet with records of my medicine and goes to the doctor with me. This helps the doctor to know if my medication needs to be altered based on how I am feeling.

Others have come along and encouraged me as well. After we moved back to the U.S., I really struggled with driving. Lancaster County has so many curves, corners, hills and sharp bends. When we would get in the car and it was my turn to drive, my son Joseph would say, "Lets pray." So we would pray. When we came to the top of the hill, he would say, "Mom we're on top of the hill, keep going. Now we're half way down, keep going, keep going." When we got to the bottom he would say, "Good job Mom. You're a good driver." He was a great encourager.

Chapter 22

Weapons to Fight Anxiety and Depression

1. Prayer

Always be ready to pray throughout the day. You don't have to be sitting or kneeling. Just keep your mind and thoughts directed towards God and keep yourself in continual conversation with Him. Let him know how you're feeling. Take a few minutes every day to sit in silence and allow Him to speak to you. The more you practice this discipline, the easier it gets to hear Him throughout your day. He longs to sit and talk with us. He longs to encourage us and tell us how much He loves us. Take time to listen, and if He convicts you of any sin, whether in the past or the present, He will forgive you and your load will be lighter. Don't be afraid to simply listen, because it is in listening that we learn to hear His voice and receive words of life from Him. Come to Him expecting to be loved and encouraged by Jesus.

2. Music

Play some upbeat worship music, or have the radio on when you are driving. I find that I have to be careful with the kind of lyrics I listen to. Even some Christian songs can lead to negative or discouraging thoughts.

3. Self Care

Take a shower, comb your hair, and put on your favorite outfit. Feeling good about yourself is half the battle in fighting anxiety and depression. When I am struggling, I do not even want to get out of bed or take a shower. Sometimes people comment on the fact that I am always dressed up. They don't know that it is part of my therapy to stay on top of anxiety and depression.

It is so easy to either wear a night gown all day or slip into that big old T-shirt that covers a multitude of sins, but the small steps of getting out of bed, taking a shower, and putting on a nice outfit can make a world of difference. Taking care of yourself, even when you don't feel like it, helps a lot. If you feel you don't even have the strength to comb your hair, ask a friend or family member to do it for you. Get a manicure, pedicure, or a massage. If you can't afford to go to a salon or spa, have a friend or family member do it for you. Relaxing and caring for yourself can relieve some of the stress that builds up anxiety. I know it is hard to ask for help but when you need it, go ahead and ask for it, and once you start feeling better, you can help someone else.

4. Light

Surround yourself with bright colors and sunshine. If the house is too dark, go out for a walk. Try to keep your house bright and cheerful. Your mind is fighting darkness, and sunshine brings in lots of light.

5. Laughter

Proverbs 17:22 says, "A cheerful heart is good medicine, but a crushed spirit dries up the bones." Look for opportunities to laugh. There are many sources of clean jokes on the internet. You can go on YouTube and search for some clean jokes to lift your spirits. Some Christian bookstores also sell funny books, DVDs and CDs. One of my favorites is Patsy Clairmont. She laughs at herself and I have found that as I learn to laugh at myself, my load seems lighter. Let me see if I can bring a smile to your face with a couple of jokes.

I'm Thirsty
Received from Troy Schwartz

A small boy is sent to bed by his father. Five minutes later: "Da-ad..."

"What?"

"I'm thirsty. Can you bring a drink of water?"

"No, you had your chance. Lights out."

Five minutes later: "Da-aaaad..."

"What?!"

"I'm *thirsty*. Can I have a drink of water?"

"I told you, *no*! If you ask again, I'll have to spank you!"

Five minutes later: "Daaaa-aaaad..."

"What!"

"When you come in to spank me, can you bring a drink of water?"

Maybe this one will do the trick.

Ice Cream
Received from ArcaMax Jokes

An elderly couple was watching television one evening. The wife said, "I am going to get a dish of ice cream now."

Kindly, the husband offered to get the ice cream for his wife. "I'll write it down so you don't forget," she said.

"I won't forget," the old gent said.

"But I want chocolate syrup and nuts on it, so I'll write it down," she replied.

"I will get you the ice cream. Don't you worry," replied the gentleman.

A few minutes later, the old man returned with bacon and eggs. His wife said, "See. I should have written it down because you forgot the toast."

Not laughing yet? Third time's the charm.

No Parking

Received from Larry

A minister parked his car in a no-parking zone in a large city because he was short of time and couldn't find a space with a meter. Then he put a note under the windshield wiper that read: "I have circled the block 10 times. If I don't park here, I'll miss my appointment. 'Forgive us our trespasses.'"

When he returned, he found a citation from a police officer along with this note: "I've circled this block for 10 years. If I don't give you a ticket, I'll lose my job. 'Lead us not into temptation.'"

6. *Positive People*

Being around people who are always complaining and grumbling will drag you down. It is so easy to find misery and there are plenty of miserable people. I have a couple of friends who are in wheel chairs, they need help to do just about everything, but oh how they laugh, tease, and thank God for a new day and for their families and friends. It makes a difference how you choose to look at life.

7. Reflection

Think through your day. If you have some unresolved issues, pray about them. You can also verbally process them with a spouse, friend, or family member. Before going to sleep, focus on the positives of the day, and the things you did well. Then, when you wake up, you're more likely to have good thoughts in your mind, instead of being burdened by the trials of the day before.

8. Grace

Give yourself grace. Don't beat yourself up for little things, or expect perfection from yourself. Give yourself permission to take a nap if you're tired. Don't feel guilty if you need to rest.

9. Exercise.

This is *very* important. When you exercise, your body releases endorphins, which are chemicals that make you feel good. Exercise is a way to combat the chemical reactions that may be causing your anxiety and depression.

10. Positive Self-Talk

When I struggle with driving I make declarations like, "I am a good driver. I have driven this way before and made it home safely, so between God and I, we can do it again." I talk to myself all the time if I am afraid. I tell myself there is nothing to fear for God Himself is with me, just as He told Joshua: "No one will be able to stand up against you all the days of your life. As I was with Moses, so I will be with you; I will never leave you nor forsake you. Be strong and courageous, because you will lead these people to inherit the land I swore to their forefathers to give them" (Joshua 1:5-6).

Sometimes when I feel panicky and start sweating and feeling like I will pass out I remember this verse: "I will not die but live, and will proclaim what the LORD has done" (Psalm 118:17).

11. Safety

Find a place where you can go and share anything and everything without any fear of judgment. It needs be a safe place where the things you share are kept confidential. Ask the Lord to lead you to a person that can be your safe place. I have a person who is a prayerful, encouraging listener and understands some of the cultural dynamics that are a part of my life.

In His book *Woman Thou Art Loosed,* T.D. Jakes (2006) writes, "The secret of being transformed from a vulnerable victim to a victorious, loving person is found in the ability to open your past to someone responsible enough to share your weakness and pain " (p. 57).

12. Outward Focus

When we struggle with mental health, it is so easy for us to always think about ourselves, our pain, and our fears, and become inward-grown. I have found that as long as I am thinking about myself and my issues all the time, I feel stuck and caught in a trap. When I become other-focused, I am able to take my eyes off of my feelings and give to others. Call someone up and pray with them. Cook a meal and invite someone over. Don't always be the receiver. Be a giver!

Chapter 23

Living Victoriously

Many times, when we have trials or sickness or a disorder, it's easy for us to become a victim, and allow our struggles to control us, instead of the other way around. God can walk with us day by day so that the disorders are not controlling our lives and making us unproductive. I have realized that the enemy would love to magnify the disorders so much that we are always playing victim instead of being victors. We can overcome because He overcame for us.

I remember the days that I would lie on the couch for hours. I couldn't read or focus, or even comb my hair. I didn't feel like doing anything, so I sat around. The more I sat around, the worse I felt, and the worse I looked, the worse I felt. I used to use the disorders as excuses for not doing the things I knew God wanted me to do. If I didn't feel like spending time with God, it was because I was depressed, if I didn't feel like cleaning the house, it was because I was depressed. This continued to be a pattern until I realized that God expects me to be a growing disciple of His, regardless of my disorders. At that point I accepted the disorder as part of my journey and I also told myself that I was not going to allow it to take over my life.

I said, "I don't feel like God is going to take this away right now, so I'm going to get up, take a shower, dress nice, go out the door, and take a walk. I'm going to start reengaging in church, and start inviting people over again. I have this disease, but I don't want this disease to have *me*." So that is exactly what I did. I still felt bad, but I decided that I wasn't going to let the way I felt dictate my life.

One day, like so many others, I woke up feeling empty and alone. I had been taking medicine, and although I didn't find out until later, the pharmacist had confused my dosage. It was a dark, dreary day, and I couldn't rally the strength to face the day. In my sorrow, I prayed, "God, where are you?" Instantly, the lyrics of the song *I Will Be Here* by Steven Curtis Chapman popped into my head. The song begins with the words, "Tomorrow morning if you wake up and the sun does not appear, I will be here."

That was the day that God sang me a song. Zephaniah 3:17 says, "The LORD your God is with you, he is mighty to save. He will take great delight in you, he will quiet you with his love, he will rejoice over you with singing." I felt He intended each of those words just for me. I gathered my strength and got out of bed for a few hours and did some dishes. The next morning was just as dark and gray as the day before, but the words to the song lingered in my mind, and I knew that God was with me.

Some of the most hopeful words in scripture are found in Isaiah 61:1-3. Each of these three verses are filled with promises from God. Meditate on these promises as you continue your journey with anxiety and depression.

"The Spirit of the Sovereign LORD is on me,
because the LORD has anointed me
to preach good news to the poor.

He has sent me to bind up the brokenhearted,
to proclaim freedom for the captives
and release from darkness for the prisoners" (Isaiah 61:1).

There are four distinct promises in this first verse. The first is that Jesus has come to bring good news to the poor. Jesus repeats these words in Luke 4, pointing to Himself as the one who has come to fulfill these scripture. We all need good news, especially those of us who struggle with anxiety and depression.

The second promise we see in Isaiah 61:1 is that Jesus has come to bind up the brokenhearted. Our hearts are broken in so many places. We feel broken-hearted when our struggle with anxiety and depression gets intense, but Jesus has come bind up our hearts. When I think of Jesus taking the pieces of our hearts and putting them back together, I cannot help but remember the Psalmist who asked the Lord to create in him a new heart. I believe that God is able to create new hearts that are not wounded by sin.

The third promise in this verse is that Jesus has come to proclaim freedom for the captives. So many people are captives to anxiety and depression as well as to sin, fear, and many other things. Jesus came to proclaim freedom for those who are captives. Anxiety and depression can suck the life out of a person and they can become completely controlled by these two vices. I find that I have to keep remembering that I do not have to allow anxiety and depression to have my life. God has allowed me to walk with this sickness, but He still expects me to continue to be His disciple and to keep growing in my walk with Him. This is a great motivation to not allow anxiety and depression to control me. I hide His promises in my heart. I sing praises to Him, pray, and forgive others, and then I trust Him with the rest of my journey every day. I am free!

The fourth promise in Isaiah 61:1, is the release from darkness for the prisoners. Anxiety and depression can feel like a major dungeon—a dark hole. Jesus has come to release us from that place. In Psalm 23:4 the psalmist declares, "Even though I walk through the valley of the shadow of death, I will fear no evil, for you are with me; your rod and your staff, they comfort me." This means that in those dark times we are not alone. God is right there with us walking beside us until we get out of the valley.

> "To proclaim the year of the LORD's favor
> and the day of vengeance of our God,
> to comfort all who mourn" (Isaiah 61:2).

In Isaiah 61:2, the Lord promises to comfort all who mourn. Sometimes anxiety and depression can feel like a never ending period of mourning. I believe that God knows it feels that way, and sent Jesus to comfort those who feel like they are in a never-ending state of mourning. He has come to comfort us. We need to relax, kick back, sit on His lap and let Him rock us to sleep as He encourages us through His word.

> "And provide for those who grieve in Zion—
> to bestow on them a crown of beauty
> instead of ashes,
> the oil of gladness
> instead of mourning,
> and a garment of praise
> instead of a spirit of despair.

> They will be called oaks of righteousness,
> a planting of the LORD
> for the display of his splendor" (Isaiah 61:3).

The first promise in verse 3 is to provide for those who grieve in Zion—to bestow on them a crown of beauty instead of ashes. Ashes are useless. They are just the remnants that are left after a fire has gone out. Maybe you had great dreams and a passion for life before you became sick with anxiety and depression. After that passion and fire goes out, all we have left is ashes. Jesus has come to trade the ashes for a crown of beauty. Sometimes it is hard to give up those ashes because it is all we know, but He is inviting us to give them up so He can bring beauty into those burned up places.

When I think about a crown of beauty, I think of beauty pageants where the woman who is deemed most beautiful is given a crown. God looked at us and decided we are beautiful, even in the midst of our struggles.

The second promise we find in Isaiah 61:3 is the promise to give the oil of joy instead of mourning. Anxiety and Depression seem to blot out all our joy. God knows this and promises to replenish us with the oil of joy. I believe He smiles and laughs and wants us to be glad instead of being in a state of mourning

The third promise in verse 3 is to give a garment of praise instead of a spirit of despair. Many people have given up on the fight against anxiety and depression. They have lost all hope of ever having a "whole" life. But Jesus has come to bring us a garment of praise instead of despair. As I wrote earlier, there is power in praise. Jesus is offering you and I a garment of praise, will you take it and cheerfully put it on?

Toward the end of Isaiah 61:3, the Lord says, "They will be called oaks of righteousness, a planting of the LORD for the display of his splendor." If we allow God to work in us, we will become righteous people and He will show His glory through us as we allow Him to take away our despair, mourning, and ashes. He will give us a new name. Instead of being those who struggle with anxiety and depression we will become those who live victoriously with anxiety and depression.

Works Cited

Benner, D. G. (2004). The *gift of being yourself: The sacred call to self-discovery.* Downers Grove, IL. IVP Books.

Byler, J. (2009). *The Art of Christian Leadership.* Lancaster, PA. Global Disciples.

Downey, D. (2004). *Don't Stop Swinging That Hammer!* Retrieved from http://www.savedhealed.com.

Jakes, T.D. (2006). *Woman Thou Art Loosed.* Shippensburg, PA. Destiny Image Publishers.

Nouwen, H. J. L. (n.d.). Personal communication from http://www.henrinouwen.org.

Omartian, S. (2001). *Lord, I Want To Be Whole: The power of prayer and scripture in emotional healing.* Nashville, TN. Thomas Nelson Incorporated.

Powerbible.com (1999-2005). Power Bible CD [computer software]. Bronson, MI. Phil Lindner Online Publishing, inc.

Testa, M. L.(n.d.). Depression. Retrieved from http://www.marytestacounseling.com on 2/9/2013.

Acknowledgements

I want to acknowledge Jesus Christ as my redeemer, who has given everything He could ever give so that I could live victoriously.

Thank you to Esther Good for supporting me in writing this book. Thank you for writing, correcting, and listening to me. Thank you for encouraging me to keep writing, even when I would have stopped and given up. I admire your quiet and gentle spirit and am blessed by your gift of writing.

Thank you to Jon Byler for reading the first manuscript and helping make good positive changes.

Thank you to Kim Myers for reading the manuscript and editing it while cheering me on.

Thank you to Linda Boll for reading the manuscript and editing it joyfully.

Thank you to Janice Martin for allowing me to use her description of the chemical reactions in the brain.

Thank you to Melanie (Byler) Nofziger for writing a forward for this book. You are a woman that I admire for your love of the Lord, family and friends. I also admire your very positive outlook on life.

About the Author

Loice Byler was born and raised in a Christian home in Kenya, East Africa. Her greatest joy is the privilege of having a relationship with Christ. She accepted Christ at an early age and later recommitted her life to Him in college.

Loice has struggled with anxiety and depression for most of her adult life. Through this struggle that she has learned very important lessons about her relationship with God.

Loice writes this book praying that it will encourage many others who struggle with mental health issues and disorders. Loice Byler, loves the Lord Jesus Christ with all her heart. She loves Him because He first loved her and gave Himself for her. It is this knowledge that has given her great hope even in the midst of suffering and pain. Loice is the Founder and President of Freedom In Him Ministries, a ministry that has the purpose of ministering mainly to women who struggle with anxiety and depression.

Loice enjoys connecting with women at retreats, conferences, mom's morning out, mother daughter banquets, and one on one prayer ministry.

Loice is married to her best friend Rev. Jon Byler. They are the proud parents of three children and they currently reside in Lancaster Pennsylvania USA

Loice would love to hear your testimony of how this book has helped you. Your questions and prayer requests are also welcome. To contact Loice, email

Loice@FreedomInHimMinistries.com.

About Freedom In Him Ministries

Freedom In Him Ministries was founded primarily to help those who struggle with anxiety and depression. Loice is available for retreats, conferences, one on one prayer ministry, and even a mom's morning out group. See Freedom In Him's web page at www.FreedomInHimMinistries.com for a list of topics that Loice speaks about. Freedom In Him also hold girls sexual purity classes, which end in a celebration of commitment. Loice would be delighted to walk with you on your journey. To contact Loice, email Loice@FreedomInHimMinistries.com.